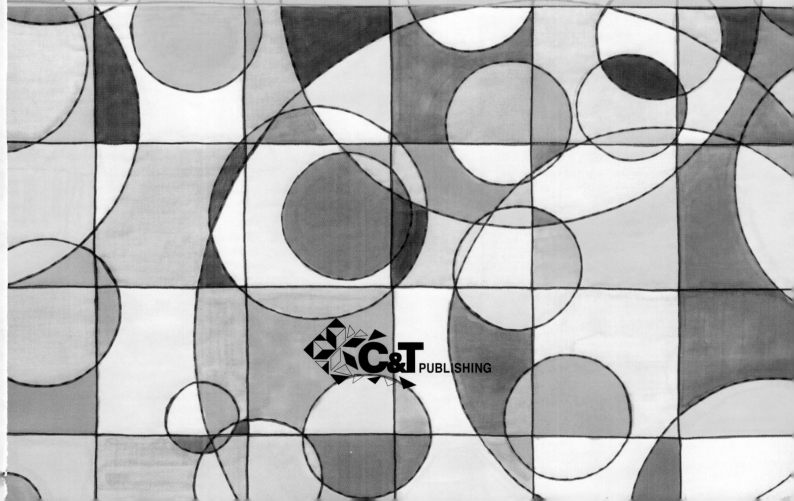

KATIE FOWLER

FOOLPROOF ART QUILTING

COLOR·LAYER·STITCH

REDISCOVER CREATIVE PLAY

C&T PUBLISHING

Text, photography, and artwork copyright © 2022 by Katie Fowler

Photography and artwork copyright © 2022 by C&T Publishing, Inc.

Publisher: Amy Barrett-Daffin

Creative Director: Gailen Runge

Acquisitions Editor: Roxane Cerda

Managing Editor: Liz Aneloski

Editor: Kathryn Patterson

Technical Editor: Debbie Rodgers

Cover/Book Designer: April Mostek

Production Coordinator: Tim Manibusan

Production Editor: Jennifer Warren

Illustrators: Valyrie Gillum, Katie Fowler, and Zinnia Heinzmann

Photography Assistant: Gabriel Martinez

Instructional photography by Katie Fowler; subjects photography by Lauren Herberg
of C&T Publishing, Inc., unless otherwise noted

Published by C&T Publishing, Inc., P.O. Box 1456, Lafayette, CA 94549

Attention Teachers: C&T Publishing, Inc., encourages the use of our books as texts for
teaching. You can find lesson plans for many of our titles at ctpub.com or contact us at
ctinfo@ctpub.com.

We take great care to ensure that the information included in our products is accurate
and presented in good faith, but no warranty is provided, nor are results guaranteed.
Having no control over the choices of materials or procedures used, neither the author
nor C&T Publishing, Inc., shall have any liability to any person or entity with respect
to any loss or damage caused directly or indirectly by the information contained in
this book. For your convenience, we post an up-to-date listing of corrections on our
website (ctpub.com). If a correction is not already noted, please contact our customer
service department at ctinfo@ctpub.com or P.O. Box 1456, Lafayette, CA 94549.

Trademark (™) and registered trademark (®) names are used throughout this book.
Rather than use the symbols with every occurrence of a trademark or registered
trademark name, we are using the names only in the editorial fashion and to the
benefit of the owner, with no intention of infringement.

Library of Congress Cataloging-in-Publication Data

Names: Fowler, Katie, 1962- author.

Title: Foolproof art quilting : color, layer, stitch; rediscover creative play / Katie Fowler.

Description: Lafayette, CA : C&T Publishing, [2022]

Identifiers: LCCN 2021048217 | ISBN 9781644031322 (trade paperback) |
ISBN 9781644031339 (ebook)

Subjects: LCSH: Art quilts--Design. | Color in art.

Classification: LCC TT835 .F693 2022 | DDC 746.46--dc23/eng/20211001

LC record available at https://lccn.loc.gov/2021048217

Printed in the USA

10 9 8 7 6 5 4 3 2 1

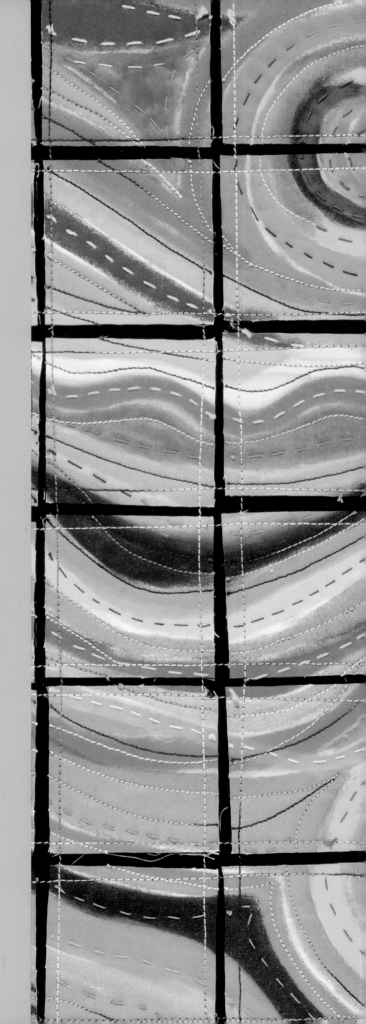

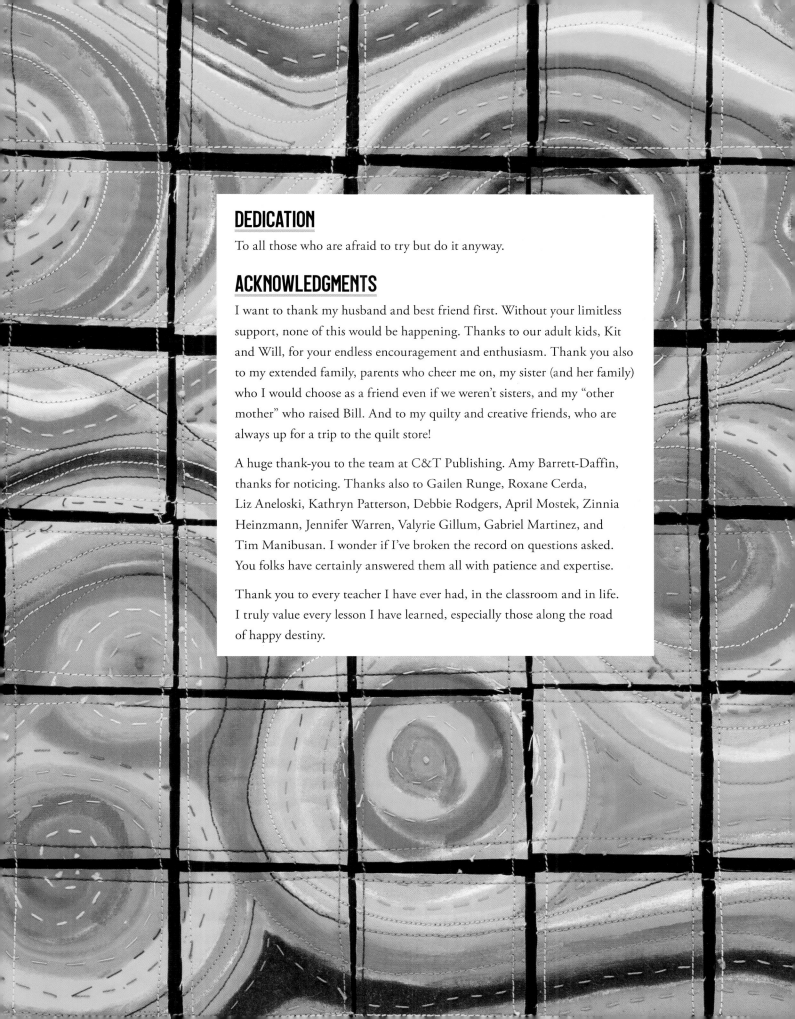

DEDICATION

To all those who are afraid to try but do it anyway.

ACKNOWLEDGMENTS

I want to thank my husband and best friend first. Without your limitless support, none of this would be happening. Thanks to our adult kids, Kit and Will, for your endless encouragement and enthusiasm. Thank you also to my extended family, parents who cheer me on, my sister (and her family) who I would choose as a friend even if we weren't sisters, and my "other mother" who raised Bill. And to my quilty and creative friends, who are always up for a trip to the quilt store!

A huge thank-you to the team at C&T Publishing. Amy Barrett-Daffin, thanks for noticing. Thanks also to Gailen Runge, Roxane Cerda, Liz Aneloski, Kathryn Patterson, Debbie Rodgers, April Mostek, Zinnia Heinzmann, Jennifer Warren, Valyrie Gillum, Gabriel Martinez, and Tim Manibusan. I wonder if I've broken the record on questions asked. You folks have certainly answered them all with patience and expertise.

Thank you to every teacher I have ever had, in the classroom and in life. I truly value every lesson I have learned, especially those along the road of happy destiny.

CONTENTS

LESSONS   76

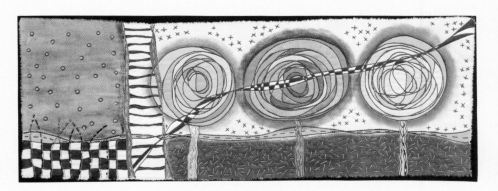

Idunn's Orchard   90

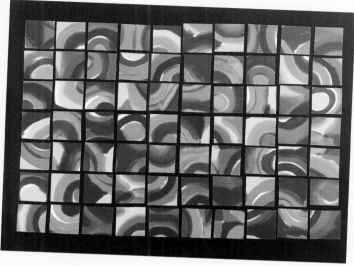

Kandinsky Kopied   98

Mad Hatter's Love Letter   100

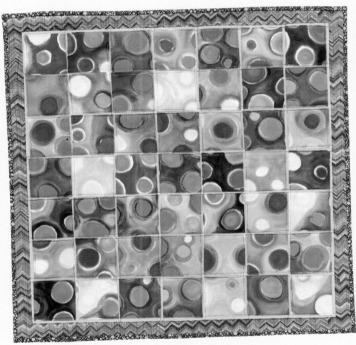

Wyrd   107

INTRODUCTION:
WHY FOOLPROOF?

Welcome to foolproof art quilting! Impossible, you say? Possible, I say. This process *is* absolutely foolproof. I guarantee it. I can guarantee it because if you don't like your painting, you can cut it up and appliqué it onto another piece of fabric. If you layer and quilt your painting, and you still don't like it, you can cut up the finished quilt and put it back together. Cut up pieces *always* look amazing. I've taught this method to a lot of adults as well as children and it is an artistic axiom (truth) that cutting it up *always* makes it look awesome.

Here's a story about cutting up a quilt. In the summer of 2014, I decided to make a quilt that would get into Quilt National or Visions. Well, long story short, not only did it not get into Quilt National, but it didn't even make it into the online show for my local guild. An email to request tickets to the taping of *The Quilt Show* prompted the editor, Lilo, to call and chat. After a few conversations, I was invited to be a featured artist on *The Quilt Show with Alex Anderson and Ricky Tims*. When discussing my creative process with the producer, she asked if I had any ideas for cutting something up that would be exciting. Of course, the 60″ × 60″ wholecloth quilt immediately came to mind.

The Color of Infinity
Photo by Katie Fowler

I did my schtick on the show. I showed Alex how I paint on fabric and Ricky how I sometimes cut stuff up. Spoiler alert: I took the 60″ × 60″ *finished* wholecloth quilt off the wall and cut it in half on the show. The audience gasped, Ricky was speechless, and my hands were shaking. Ricky asked me if I were mad at that quilt. I told him I was not, but that I had thought it would make me famous. His reply? "Oh, it's going to make you famous, all right." Well, I'm not famous, but I have enjoyed a wonderful just-busy-enough national teaching career since the airing of that show.

We had to do a little debriefing with the audience after taping wrapped. They were truly shocked by the fact that I cut up that finished quilt. Here are some important points about creativity and why it was really all right for me to cut up a quilt I had worked on for almost a year. First, I didn't love the finished quilt. I liked it, but it didn't speak to my heart, I think, because I didn't make

From Mandelbrot to Madness

it with my heart. I made it to get into Quilt National. Someone had told me Quilt National judges like "big," so I made a quilt bigger than I like to make, and I made it so others would like it—not from my heart.

Second, the true joy of creativity is in the creative process. If we love what we've made, that's icing on the cake, but what I really enjoy is the planning, problem solving, and doing in all its messy and uncertain glory. I'm not sure I've ever made a "masterpiece," but the pieces I like the best

are the ones for which I've followed my heart, allowing the process to be the reward. Finally, and most importantly, my intention in my studio is *not* to create a masterpiece that will hang in a museum but to lose myself and spend time without time in my creative space. I want to be in that space where time passes and I don't notice. I want to be totally absorbed in what I'm doing. Psychologist Mihaly Csikszentmihalyi calls this *flow*. Flow is the state when the challenge perfectly matches the skill of the creative.

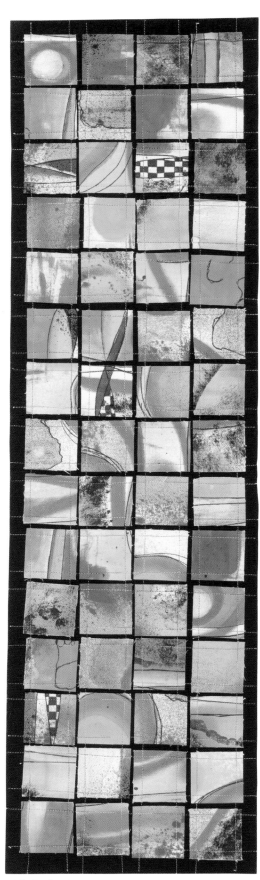

Make Evident 1

Make Evident 2

I hope you have experienced flow. If you haven't, this book will help you find it. If you have, you know exactly what I'm talking about. Maybe you have experienced flow but have lost it. That's okay. I can help you find it again. As you explore the materials and techniques in this book, remember your intention. It isn't likely that you will paint a masterpiece your first try. When you spill paint (done that), bobble your pen (done that), or make a mark you really wish you could erase (done that, too), remember that you can cut it up when you're finished and it's going to look good.

These pieces are called *Make Evident* because they were made from a painting that wasn't a painting but a piece of fabric I used to demonstrate materials and techniques. They were unlovely pieces, really more like rags than paintings. They do not look like rags after cutting them up and appliquéing them to black wool felt.

Take the pressure off. Enjoy yourself. Creativity is supposed to be fun! Why else would we buy all these materials and spend all this time learning new skills? This is a leisure activity, so if you aren't having fun, I suggest you find another way to spend your free time. Again, take the pressure off, leave perfectionism and comparison at the door, and for the love of all things colorful, have fun!

Magic Creativity

Being creative is not a superpower. It isn't something that some people are born with while others aren't. Being creative is part of the human condition. If you are human, and I assume you are, you are creative. It comes with your head. It's part of your DNA. Here are some common examples of how you might be creative: Have you formed a sentence with multiple words? Have you ever used your imagination? If you answered yes to either question, you are creative. Please don't tell me you don't have a creative bone in your body.

At the beginning of one of the most wonderful and terrifying stories I can remember reading as a child, Alice is sitting under a tree, bored out of her mind, barely able to keep her eyes open. She spies a rabbit in a waistcoat. She just has to follow the rabbit. Join me on a creative journey. Let's follow Alice down that rabbit hole.

So, why is it so hard? Just pick up your pen or your paintbrush and get started. Why are you afraid? What is stopping you from going to that place where time ceases to exist and you completely lose yourself to your passion? You know the place I'm talking about. You love it there! Why is it easier to do laundry rather than … *wait, what*!?! Did you say afraid? I'm not afraid to create; why would I be afraid?

THE CREATIVITY CRUSHERS

What is it that scares us? That is the big question. To help me answer that question, I've named the creativity crushers that most often keep me from creative adventure.

To begin, meet Dobie Doubter. Dobie politely asks me if I'm sure I know what I'm doing. Dobie cautions me to be safe and careful. "Are you sure? Oh, be careful!"

Next is the more aggressive and meaner Bully B*tch. She is the queen bee and loves to put others down. "Wow ... What? You cannot be serious. Really?"

Another foe is the Fluke Flinger. This pesky bug takes every success I've ever had and expertly turns it into a fluke. "Yes, that was nice, but it was a fluke. You'll never be able to do anything like that again."

Finally, the Poser Dozer constantly reminds me that I don't really know what I'm doing. "You are such a poser, such an imposter! You don't know what you're doing!"

What in the world does this have to do with creativity? Well, the creativity crushers get the lizard brain going. The lizard brain can only do few things, like fight or fly.

Because the lizard brain doesn't have the capacity to evaluate fear, it automatically goes to work, even if the fear is ridiculous! Once the lizard brain is going, our creativity is completely shut down. Many of us are afraid and don't even know it. Fear tells us we can't lose if we don't play; we can't fail if we don't try. Now isn't that just silly?

Go ahead! Don't be afraid! Laugh at those creativity crushers. Grin at them like the Cheshire Cat would.

PERFECTIONISM AND THE QUEEN OF HEARTS

Alice spends most of *Alice's Adventures in Wonderland* looking for the lovely garden she glimpsed when she first fell down the rabbit hole. I like to think of that elusive garden as that place where I find myself in the "creative groove."

Remember when Alice finally gets through the door to the garden and finds the gardeners painting the white roses red? Well, they are painting those roses because of the Queen of Hearts' perfectionism.

Just like a spoiled child, the Queen of Hearts must have everything exactly how she wants it, or she throws a tantrum. This is a good illustration of how perfectionism works in the creative process.

Perfectionism kills the creative flow just like the Queen's arbitrary and frequent order of "Off with her head!"

Perfectionism is deadly because it kills the creative flow. I, for one, am totally incapable of making anything close to perfect. I embrace the blob and value my imperfection. My imperfection is mine; it makes my art *mine*. If perfect were my goal, I would change mediums. I certainly wouldn't be painting on fabric. It doesn't lend itself to perfectionism. Paints bleed. Drips and spills happen.

Just like painting the white roses red won't really make them red roses, perfectionism won't really help the creative process. So, what's to be done? We can't just change from a white rose to a red rose, now can we? We need to accept ourselves just the way we are. If the roses are white, learn to love white roses. It has been my experience that acknowledging the counterproductive thoughts and moving ahead anyway gets me where I'm going in a much happier state.

Here's a secret: Nobody's head ever gets chopped off in Alice's adventures. Imperfection doesn't kill. Embrace the blob and learn to love white roses!

COMPARISON AND THE CAUCUS RACE

Let's talk about comparison, shall we? This little mental maneuver is probably one of the most devastating and crippling things we can do to ourselves. It is quite common. Some of us do it more than others. Let's look at a common example.

Comparison is sitting in a class and looking around at others' work and measuring up how your work compares. No matter how you do it ("Wow, mine is so much better than everyone else's," or "OMG, I'm mortified! Mine looks like a 4-year-old did it compared to everyone else!"), comparison is totally negative.

After Alice gets out of the pool of tears, she happens upon the caucus race. The caucus race is a perfect simile for comparison. In the story, a racecourse is marked out in the sand, a circle. All the animals and Alice take a place on the circle and begin racing one another. After some time passes, the Dodo announces that the race is over. It is totally impossible to determine a winner.

Everyone starts from a different place at a different time. Who is ahead and who is behind? Every time you compare yourself to someone else, you are participating in your own little caucus race: running in circles, going nowhere, with no way to win.

Comparison is not the same thing as competition. I know many successful creative people who thrive on competition. Good, clean competition helps hone skills and confidence by consciously putting work out there to be judged. It is a choice, a mutually agreed upon relationship. Competition is a clearly marked racecourse with a well-defined start and finish line. That's cool!

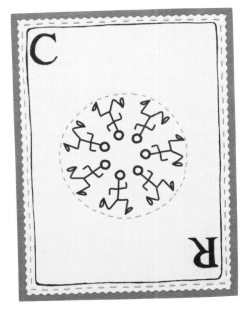

Comparison has no start, no finish, no beginning, no end—it's just running around in meaningless circles, going nowhere. Comparison is an exchange. If you are better than me, then I am worse. I exchange my worth for yours. It is totally unproductive. And the thing about comparison is that it never ends. There will always be someone better and someone worse. It's all random.

For me, self-acceptance is paramount to my success and happiness. If my self-acceptance is in good shape, I don't compare myself to others. I am happy with who and how I am. That feels so much better than all that measuring and weighing. I have had to change my self-talk. Now comparison isn't any fun. It makes me feel icky inside.

It has taken me most of my life so far, but today I don't spend much time or energy running in comparison caucus races. Of course, I jump into the circle occasionally, but I don't stay there long. It just doesn't serve me or my creative process.

It's a caucus race. We all start and stop at different times and places. No one wins; everybody loses. It sucks all the joy out of everything: the group, the creative process, and the feeling of accomplishment. Stop it. Just stop it. Now that you know comparison for what it really is, you can begin to recognize when you are comparing. Comparison is a bad habit, and it can be changed.

SIX IMPOSSIBLE THINGS BEFORE BREAKFAST: FIGHTING RESISTANCE

Resistance is a stealth killer of creativity. It keeps us from doing what we really want to do. When in resistance, we say things like, "I just can't," "I don't really want to," and "You can't make me!" We also ask heartbreaking questions like, "Why can't I commit to what feeds my soul?" Being in resistance feels frustrating, exhausting, and oh so terrible. It's like being in the doldrums. Nothing will get you moving again. There is no wind to fill your creative sails.

When Alice is in Looking Glass Land, she's having a conversation with the White Queen.

"I can't believe THAT!" said Alice. > *(resistance)*

"Can't you?" the Queen said in a pitying tone.
"Try again: draw a long breath, and shut your eyes." > *(coaxing, list making, and so on)*

Alice laughed. "There's no use trying," she said.
"One *can't* believe impossible things." > *(more resistance)*

"I daresay you haven't had much practice," said the Queen.
"When I was your age, I always did it for half-an-hour a day.
Why sometimes I've believed as many as six impossible things before breakfast."

So, believe six impossible things before breakfast. Cute, but what has that got to do with me? I'm glad you asked. Think back to your childhood (a happy memory, please). What did you like to play? My favorites were Barbie, school, and artist. I cannot ever remember being in resistance when my friend Kim and I would play artist. Actually, we didn't play artist. We believed in our hearts of hearts that we were artists. I specifically remember experimenting with oil pastels and rubbing alcohol resulting in the most amazing cloudscapes. No resistance!

Sometimes, after we grow up, we forget how to abandon ourselves to something we love. When the Queen was Alice's age, "seven and a half exactly," she practiced imagining impossible things. The Queen taps into her inner child. She finds her imaginative voice that ignores the sensible voice. We can do this too when resistance shows up. Find an impossible thing to believe and go back to that happy place where you knew no resistance.

So, here are six not-so-impossible things you can practice right now. Don't wait until tomorrow before breakfast.

KISS: Keep It Small, Sweetheart! Go look at your supplies. Get reacquainted with them.

KILL: Keep It Light, Lovey! Keep it fun. Remember, we aren't aiming for perfection. Turn on some dance music and spin to the music of your uniqueness!

KARS: Kick Ass, Rock Star! Just do it! Sheer determination beats resistance every time, just like rock crushes scissors every time.

KIT: Keep In Touch! Call a friend. Go to a guild meeting. Take a class. Creativity thrives on community, except of course when it doesn't.

KTD: Klose The Door! Sometimes we just need to close the door, turn off the phone, and power down the computer. Creativity thrives on solitude, except of course when it doesn't.

KYIK: Kuddle Your Inner Kid! Remember what it felt like to do something without resistance.

I've never met a human being who has never experienced some form of resistance. Even those superhuman, overly organized, hyper-efficient ones. We all experience resistance. Just take some time to imagine six impossible things, before breakfast if possible. Go on; do it. You owe it to yourself.

"IT'S A POOR SORT OF MEMORY THAT ONLY WORKS BACKWARDS": PROCRASTINATION

The White Queen says, "The rule is jam to-morrow and jam yesterday—but never jam to-day." Procrastination feels like that to me. There is always tomorrow, problem is … tomorrow never comes.

> "It must come sometimes to jam to-day," Alice objected.
>
> "No, it can't," said the Queen. "It's jam every *other* day: today isn't any *other* day, you know."

Procrastination, like the jam rule, is very hard to fight. There are people on the planet who don't procrastinate; I even know a few of them. I also know a whole boatload of people who do procrastinate.

Procrastination is so common on the creative journey because … *duh*! Creative pursuits are hard. Creativity is unknowable, undefinable, and completely unreliable. We all know the feeling of entering our creative space and having the juices just flow. We also know the feeling of showing up to our space and staring at the blank piece of fabric.

"Jam yesterday, jam to-morrow, but *never* jam to-day." The problem with true procrastination is that tomorrow never comes for some people. That's more than a problem, that's tragic.

So, what if you want to jam today? The trick that works absolutely the best for me is a deadline. I love deadlines. Deadlines are my friend. A deadline holds my feet to the fire in a way nothing else can. This is because a deadline gives me permission to spend time, a lot of time, doing what I love.

Permission? I don't need no stinkin' permission! Yes, I do. Sad to say, I don't always feel like it's okay to spend hours losing track of time and feeding my soul. It feels selfish. It has taken me a long time to feel okay to jam … *today*!

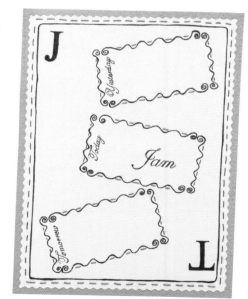

Another sneaky way for me to jam today is to use the Kaizen-Muse small steps. The small step that helps me the most is to have my morning cup of coffee in my studio. My interest will often be sparked, and I'll be off and running. What small step can you take?

Finally, make your memory work forward. The White Queen tells Alice, "It's a poor sort of memory that only works backwards." Remember tomorrow after you've spent some good quality time with your creative endeavor. I use this trick all the time. Just keep it positive; when it's negative, it's called worry. Sound crazy? It really isn't any different than worry, which most of us do naturally, except it's positive. New agers call it *manifesting*.

It must come sometimes to art today. Make today one of the *other* days, not yesterday and not tomorrow. Just do it.

CREATIVE CHAOS AND A MAD TEA PARTY

> "Why is a raven like a writing desk?"
>
> "You mean you can't take less," said the Hatter; "it's very easy to take more than nothing."

This is nonsensical chaos. Alice has enough and leaves the party. This is one time we are not following Alice's lead. We are not going to leave the party. We are going to enjoy it for all its crazy nonsense.

This nonsense is called *creative chaos*, and it's part of the process. The ideas come flooding in, too many to keep track. Or one idea comes flooding, too precious or complicated to start. The techniques keep swirling around; the materials are beckoning from the art supply store. During creative chaos, my studio can go from a relatively organized workspace to an absolute explosion. Or not—I can have too many thoughts and ideas to even think about reaching for materials.

Creative chaos is when most people quit. They leave the party. In fact, the statistic is something like 80 percent. Why do 80 percent quit? Because it's hard! It's hard to figure out how to start something, or if you've started, it's hard to figure out what to do next. Probably the hardest part for most creatives is finishing. In fact, I'm fairly confident that a support group for flailing, failing-to-finish creative types would fill up in minutes. Why? Because it's hard to finish.

If you can get through the first bit of frustration and get started, kudos! I know more than a handful of people (and I've been included in the group) who just love to go buy everything they need for a new project. They spend lots of money on supplies and tools, books and instructional videos, and sometimes even classes. They carry their cache into the studio, filled with visions of what the tea party will look like, and at the first unanswerable riddle, they bolt. We've talked about the reasons this happens. What I want to say now is that this feeling of chaos and not knowing what to do next is part of the process.

Embrace the chaos. Enjoy the perplexities. Creative problem-solving is one of my favorite parts of the process. If you must, look around your workspace and shake your head in frustration, hopelessness, or confusion. Do what you need to do. Just don't stop! Be in that small percent that doesn't quit.

You've been on an artist's journey through Wonderland. You have been exposed to some tools to help you along your creative quest. I hope you will grin at fear and let go of perfectionism. When we meet, you will introduce yourself as an artist, dancer, or writer … whatever it is you do. You won't compare your unique greatness to anyone else, ever. You will practice believing six impossible things before breakfast and always remember forward. And promise me you won't leave the party before the cake!

So, "why is a raven like a writing desk?" I have no idea. The important thing is that you can't do less if you do nothing.

It is very easy to do more than nothing.

COLOR THEORY:
A TOOL, NOT A RULE

Mad Hatter's Bunco Party

I love color—always have, always will. Sometimes I have a favorite color; sometimes I like them all the same. Color evokes moods, memories, and feelings for me. I know I'm not alone. Color is, in my opinion, one of the most valuable gifts of nature.

Isaac Newton gave us the science of color when he split white light through a prism. Physicists, ophthalmologists, and artists have been adding to that basic science since the seventeenth century.

Here's the disclaimer: I am *not* a color expert. I don't have a good understanding of how the cones in our eyes work or why we see color like we do. What I do understand is how color works as well as how colors work together.

The very best way to learn about color is to use it! This book will cover the basics, so you know why things work and why they don't. Then it's up to you. Color away, experiment, and learn what you love.

> *Remember:* Color theory is a tool, *not* a rule!

HUE

Hue is the art-school word for *color*. When you ask, "What color is it?" you are really asking, "What hue is it?"

The standard color wheel is made up of 12 hues:

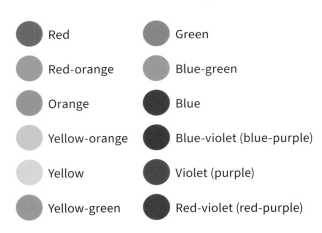

- Red
- Red-orange
- Orange
- Yellow-orange
- Yellow
- Yellow-green
- Green
- Blue-green
- Blue
- Blue-violet (blue-purple)
- Violet (purple)
- Red-violet (red-purple)

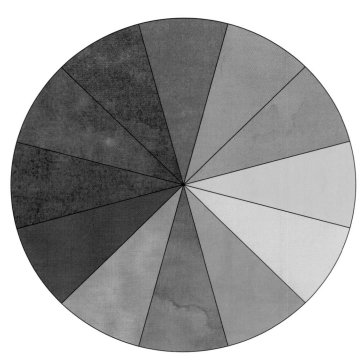

The hues are sorted into 3 main categories: *primary colors*, *secondary colors*, and *tertiary colors*. When you understand these categories, you will better understand the color wheel. Let's start with the basics.

Primary Colors

Rumor has it that you can mix any color using the 3 primary colors … and this rumor is true. If you don't want to buy every color (though I personally don't understand why you wouldn't), you can buy the primaries and mix any other color you want.

The *primary colors* are:

- Red
- Yellow
- Blue

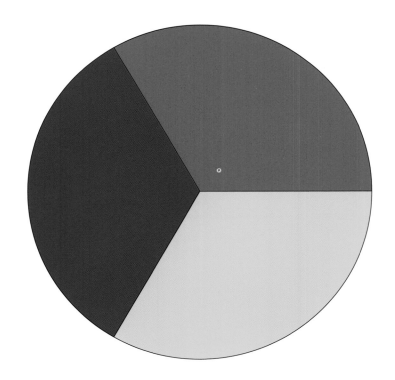

Secondary Colors

When we mix 2 primary colors together,
we get *secondary colors*.

Red   +   Yellow   =   Orange

Red   +   Blue   =   Violet

Blue   +   Yellow   =   Green

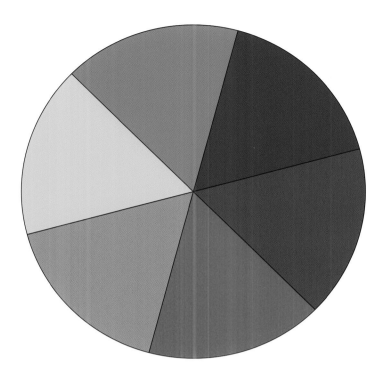

Tertiary Colors

When we mix a primary color with a
secondary color, we get *tertiary colors*.

Red   +   Orange   =   Red-orange

Yellow   +   Orange   =   Yellow-orange

Yellow   +   Green   =   Yellow-green

Blue   +   Green   =   Blue-green

Blue   +   Violet   =   Blue-violet

Red   +   Violet   =   Red-violet

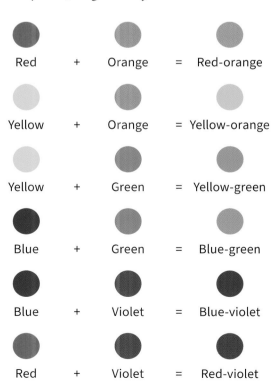

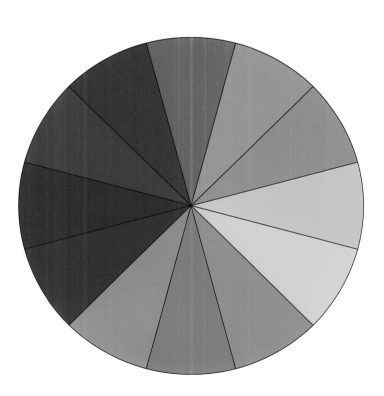

SATURATION

Now that you have a bit of understanding about the hues around the color wheel (which we probably should call a *hue wheel*), let's talk about saturation. *Saturation* is the word we use to describe the intensity of a color (the word *bright* comes to mind). Technically, the saturation of a color is the degree to which it differs from white. The most saturated colors completely cover the white page and the least saturated allow for a lot of the white page to show.

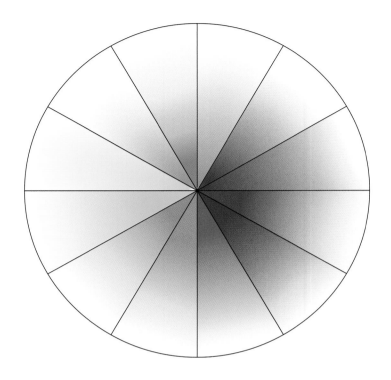

VALUE

Value is the relative degree of lightness or darkness of a color (hue). Value is achieved by adding white, black, or gray to any color. We use three terms to describe value in art:

Tint describes a color with *white* added. *Shade* describes a color with *black* added. *Tone* describes a color with *gray* (white and black) added.

Variation in value is often overlooked and can be the difference between a successful project and one that misses the mark.

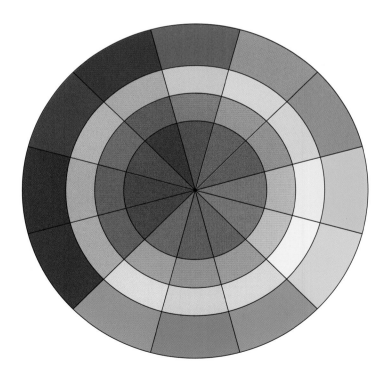

GRAY SCALE

Another way to look at value is to use the gray scale. The gray scale can have a few or many shades of gray. This illustration really illustrates how black and white affect the pure hue.

The following chart was colored as listed, blending various combinations of black and white with colors (hues).

HUE	WHITE (TINT)	WHITE + BLACK (TONE)	WHITE = BLACK (TONE)	BLACK + WHITE (TONE)	BLACK (SHADE)

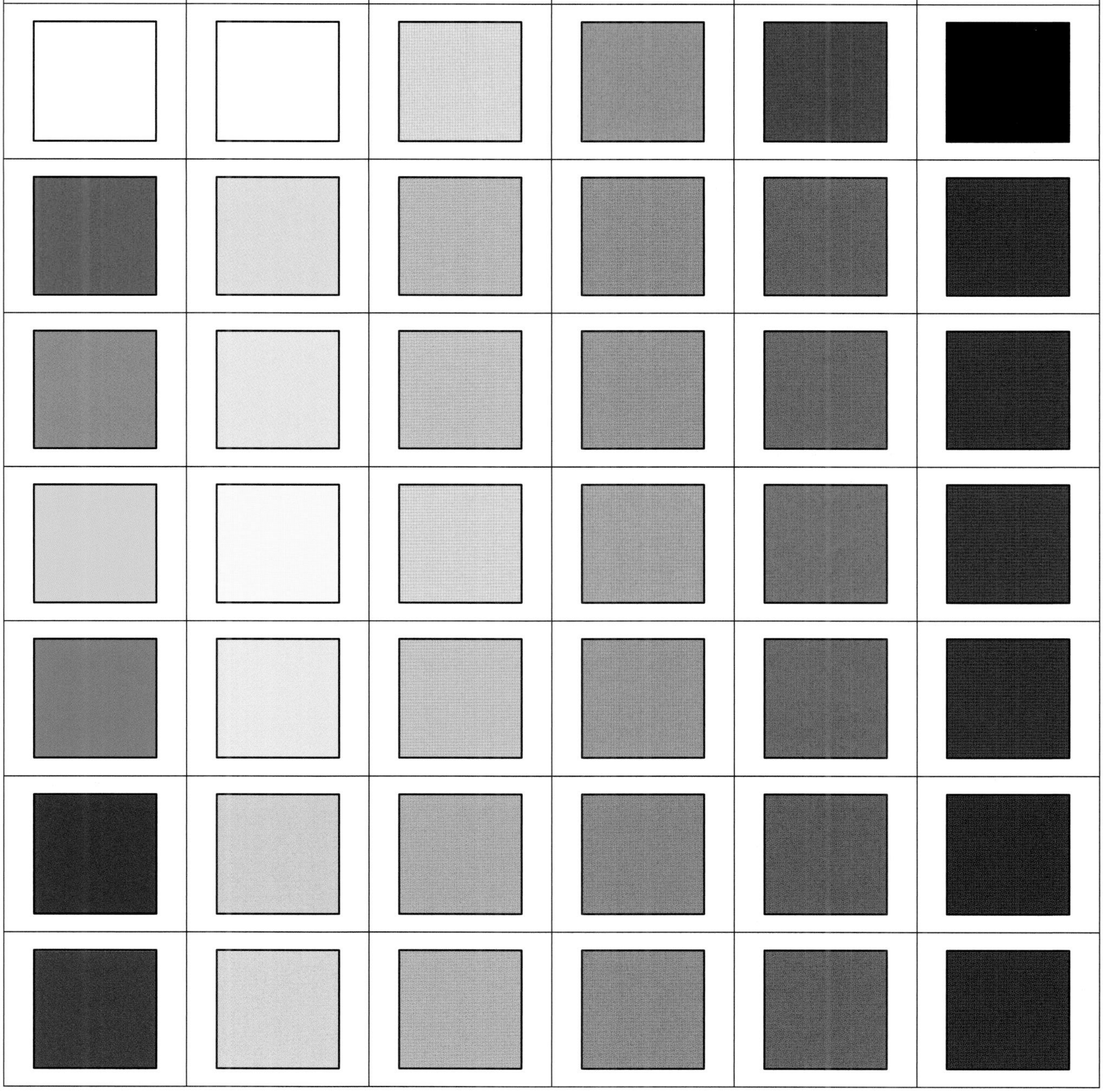

TEMPERATURE

Colors can evoke a feeling of temperature. There are warm colors and cool colors. A skilled mix of temperatures can make a stunning combination. Using only either warm or cool colors can create a feeling of specific moods.

Warm Colors

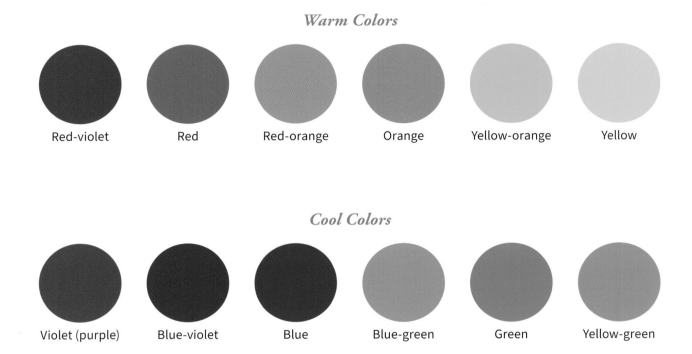

| Red-violet | Red | Red-orange | Orange | Yellow-orange | Yellow |

Cool Colors

| Violet (purple) | Blue-violet | Blue | Blue-green | Green | Yellow-green |

An overall cool palette with a splash of heat, or vice versa, can be a stunning combination.

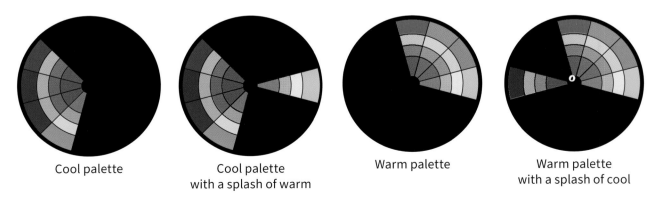

| Cool palette | Cool palette with a splash of warm | Warm palette | Warm palette with a splash of cool |

COLOR RELATIONSHIPS

Visually, colors depend on the colors around and next to them.

Look at the large green square and the large blue square (at right). It's hard to believe, but the small square in the middle of each of these large green and blue squares is the same color blue. But it looks bluer on the green background and greener on the blue background!

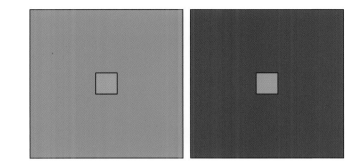

Complementary Versus Analogous

Notice in the green square (at right) how vibrant the red looks. That's because green and red are *complementary* colors, colors that are opposite each other on the color wheel. The same red dot seems to be absorbed by the orange square. That's because they are *analogous* colors, colors that are next to each other on the color wheel.

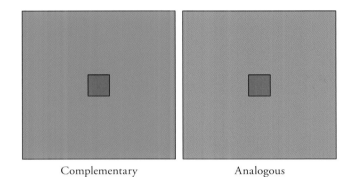

Complementary   Analogous

This image is another good example of how colors depend on the colors around them.

The 2 small squares are identical in size and color.

The blue and violet blends with the blue in the red-violet, causing it to look redder. The red and orange blend with the red in the red-violet, causing it to look bluer.

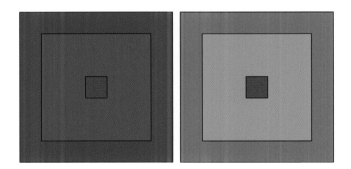

Neutrals & Color Relationships

Colors also behave differently when they are surrounded by different neutrals. Notice the difference in vibrancy when surrounded by black, gray, or white.

PRIMARY   SECONDARY

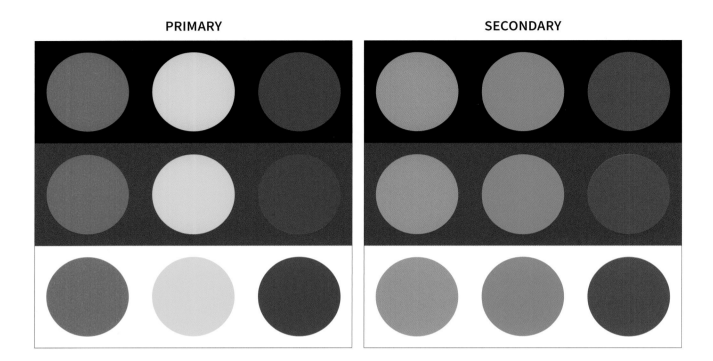

TERTIARY

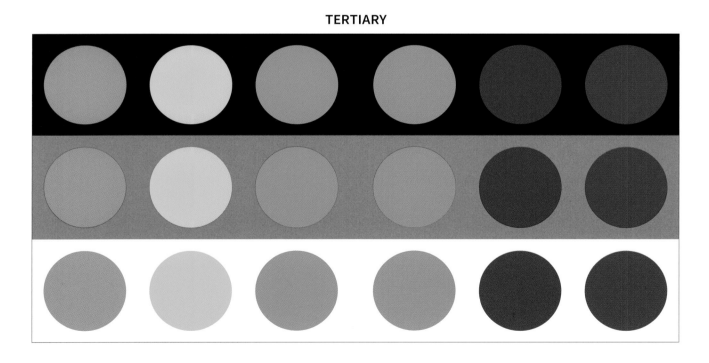

COLOR CHORDS, COMBINATIONS, OR "GREATEST HITS"

Color theorists have used the color wheel in many ways. The way most creatives use the wheel is to determine color chords (Johannes Itten), combinations, or "greatest hits" (me).

When Isaac Newton split the white light into the color spectrum using the prism, he later put the spectrum back through the prism and the colors blended into white light. With this knowledge in mind, Newton postulated that if we were to spin a color wheel fast enough, the colors would blend to a neutral gray. Guess what? It's true that if we mix all the colors on the color wheel together, they blend to make gray!

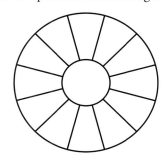

Don't believe me? Try it! Color the color wheel and add all the colors to the circle in the middle and see for yourself that all the hues combined create gray.

Color Combinations

I encourage you to get a color wheel and use it. You will learn how to use the color wheel to its best advantage.

Remember: The color wheel is a *tool*, *not* a rule!

Remember to have fun with color. And what could be more fun than playing with color? In color, like art, there is a correct way to look at things. This is the objective side of color. It helps to know the objective side of things, but it is way more fun to use the tools of color. Ultimately, make your own subjective choices. There is no wrong or right when we are choosing what we like.

We'll explore these combinations: direct complement, triad, split complement, tetrad, double complement, double-double complement, double-split complement, double triad, analogous complement, analogous, monochromatic, and neutral. Some are "real" combinations used in traditional color study; others are my own invention.

My favorite quote about color is from Freddie Moran, the quilter who mastered the most amazing use of color: "10 colors don't work; 100 colors do. Red is neutral."

This is the basic idea around color combinations that work. Here's a tidbit of science: Our brains combine colors for us. The calmest color is a neutral gray. When we combine colors that easily blend to a neutral gray, it is a pleasing combination. That's it—that's all I understand. It has something to do with the cones in our eyes and how they perceive color.

DIRECT COMPLEMENT (*IAMBIC PENTAMETER*)

A traditional combination, a *direct complement* is a color and its opposite on the color wheel. These 2 colors balance each other in temperature. 2 intense complements can be very stimulating; sports teams often choose complementary colors for this reason. This combination has 2 lead singers and no backup singers.

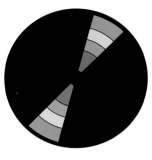

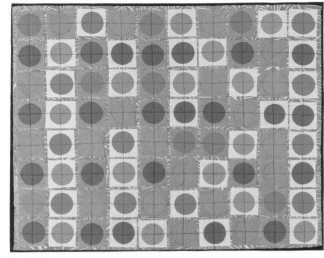

Iambic Pentameter

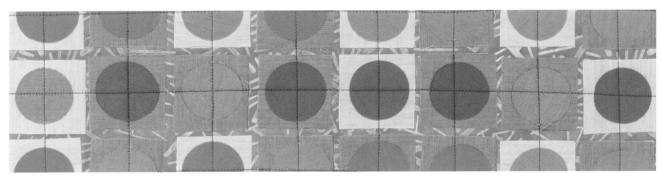

TRIAD (*THREE STACKS*)

A traditional combination, a *triad* is made of 3 evenly spaced colors on the wheel. This combination can be quite vibrant. This color combination should be carefully balanced. It often works best to choose one color as the lead singer and let the other 2 colors be supporting band members.

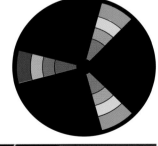

Three Stacks

SPLIT COMPLEMENT (*SOLAR FLARE*)

A traditional combination, the *split complement* uses a base color and the 2 colors next to its complement. This color scheme is popular because it is so easy to use. It has the vibrancy of a complementary combination but less tension. In this combination, there are 3 singers, none of which is the lead.

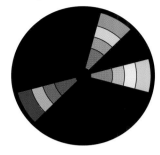

Solar Flare

TETRAD (*CHEBA CHECKERS*)

A traditional combination, a *tetrad* has 2 sets of complementary colors arranged in a square on the color wheel—2 sets of evenly spaced complements. It is wise to pay attention to warm and cool colors in a tetrad. This is a rich combination, and like the triad, it works best with a lead color and 3 supporting colors because the colors are evenly spaced.

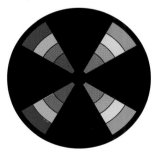

Cheba Checkers

DOUBLE COMPLEMENT (*SUNSHINE KINGDOM*)

A traditional combination, a *double complement* is also a tetrad but is arranged more like a rectangle. In other words, there are 2 sets of complements separated by 1 color between. Another rich combination, a double complement is easy to use. If it isn't working, choose a color lead and let the other 3 colors support it.

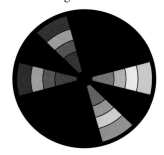

Sunshine Kingdom

DOUBLE-DOUBLE COMPLEMENT (*CABBAGES*)

This is my own name for 2 adjacent set of complements. This combination is vibrant and exciting. All of the players in this combination can share center stage.

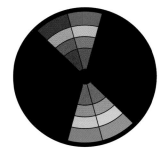

Cabbages

DOUBLE-SPLIT COMPLEMENT (*LAIR OF THE LAMB*)

This traditional combination starts with a split complement and adds a color to each of the split complements. Like the split complement, this combination is easy to use and doesn't need a lead color.

Lair of the Lamb

DOUBLE TRIAD (*FUZZY'S HEART*)

For this combination, start with a triad and add the adjacent triad. This combination is an example of how, when it comes to color parties, the more the merrier! Easy to use, this combination can be an ensemble and doesn't need a lead color.

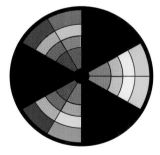

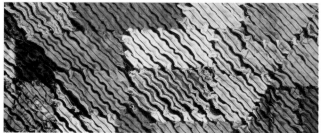

Fuzzy's Heart

ANALOGOUS COMPLEMENT
(*LAVA AND LEPRECHAUNS*)

I know we're not supposed to have favorites, but this is mine. For this traditional combination, choose one color, its complement, and the 2 or 3 colors adjacent. This combination always sings. There is a natural lead color in the complement, but all colors can be used in any proportion.

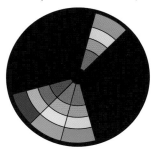

Lava and Leprechauns

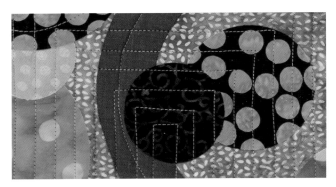

ANALOGOUS (*CONTEMPT PRIOR TO INVESTIGATION*)

This traditional combination, used in color study, is the calming voice of the color wheel. *Analogous colors* are 3–5 adjacent colors. This combination is often found in nature. Value and saturation can be important to making an analogous color combination work.

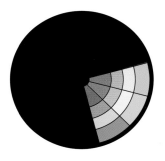

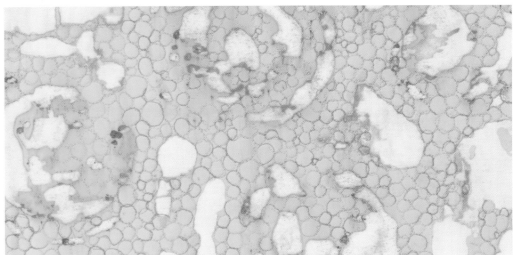

Contempt Prior to Investigation

MONOCHROMATIC
(*TANGERINE*)

This is the solo act of the traditional color combinations—just one color in all its different iterations.

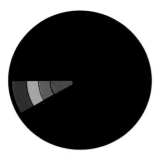

Tangerine

NEUTRAL
(*PRAIRIE SKYLINE*)

This is the absence of color.

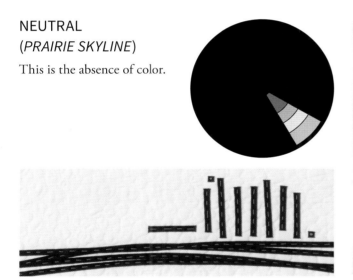

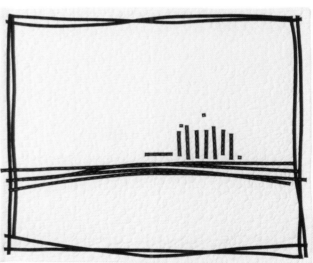

Prairie Skyline

Take the time to play with your own colors. That is how we really learn!

Remember, color theory is a tool, not a rule. Don't be limited by color theory! Use it when you want to or need to, and go with your heart the rest of the time. My experience is that the more I play with color theory and color wheel combinations, the less I need color theory and color wheel combinations. People often comment on my use of color, and I truly believe that I have developed a sense of color by using (and failing with) many different color combinations.

COMPOSITION AND DESIGN:
PUTTING IT ALL TOGETHER

I am of two minds about this chapter. I don't want anyone to read this information and feel like it's a set of rules. Like color theory, I view composition and design as tools, not rules. When you begin to see like an artist, you will see interesting inspiration all around you. Pay attention. These are great starting points for art quilts, both painted and pieced. We don't all have to look like artists, but we should try to see like artists.

ELEMENTS OF DESIGN

Most art classrooms will have a poster on the wall explaining the "elements" of design. I like to think about this list of seven things as a toolbox of considerations when making art.

Line is exactly what it sounds like. When you see a line in any artwork, that is an example of this element of design. Line is a tool many artists use to move the eye of the viewer across the artwork. Our eyes naturally follow a line. When you start to really notice your world, you will see examples of line everywhere. Line can be straight, curved, dotted, broken, thick, or thin—or a combination of the above.

Like line, *shape* is everywhere you look. I challenge you to look anywhere and not see a shape. Examples include the circular top of a mug, the rectangle of a desktop, and the triangle and octagon shapes of street signs. When shape is used in art, it provides interesting stopping points for our eye. Shape can be distinct, overlapping, geometric, or organic.

Think of a ball or a cube. A *form* is three-dimensional. Of course, we can't really paint three dimensions, but form in artwork mimics or illustrates three dimensions. Picture the cylinder of a spool of thread, the cube shape of a box of tissue, or the sphere shape of a ball.

I discussed *color* extensively in the previous chapter. As an element of design, it refers to the hue (color), saturation, value, and temperature. For most of us, it is our favorite element of design and possibly the most noticed.

Quilters love *texture*. This is the tactile part of art. Some artwork has actual texture while other artwork only implies texture. In painting, we can add texture with visible brush strokes, pattern, or my favorite, stitch.

Space refers to the areas around, within, or between images. Positive space can be the line, shape, or form. Negative space can be the space around the line, shape, or form. Negative space is effective for emphasis and as a place for the viewer to rest the eye.

Value is the lightness or darkness of a color. As an element of design, value is used for emphasis, perspective, and interest.

PRINCIPALS OF DESIGN

If the elements of design are the tools we use to make art, the principals are the instructions for how to use the tools effectively. All design principals can be applied to all design elements. Again, these instructions are tools, not rules.

Balance refers to the visual weight in an artwork. The human brain likes balance. It can be symmetrical (both sides are the same), radial (building from the center), or asymmetrical (2 sides are different but still have the same visual weight).

When 2 things are strikingly different from one another, they are high in *contrast*. Contrasting elements in art are attention grabbers. The most obvious contrast is black and white. This is a contrast in value (light versus dark). Contrast can be created using color and complementary colors have the highest contrast to one another. Shapes can provide contrast as well. One different shape among many similar shapes will create a focal point. This is true of the other elements of design as well.

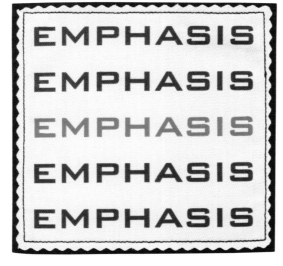

Like contrast, *emphasis* creates a focal point that draws the eye to particular areas of the artwork.

Movement refers to how the eye moves through a piece of art. The artist can manipulate how a viewer sees an artwork by using the elements to create movement.

A *pattern* decorates a piece of art. A pattern is made of elements (line, shape, and so on) that repeat in a predictable way. The pattern can be made using any of the elements of design. The key is that it repeats in a predictable way. A pattern can be organic, like my checkerboard grid, or very formal and measured.

Scale is the relative size of an element in an artwork. Think of fabrics with large-scale prints and fabrics with small-scale prints. My favorite use of scale in artwork is when 2 objects are represented in different scales. For example, a broom sweeping up a building. I played with scale in my self-portraits of Copenhagen (page 127), Florence (page 137), and Rome (page 137).

Unity describes when all elements in an artwork are harmonious. Although soothing, too much unity can be boring. Variety within elements adds interest to the composition.

So, now what? How do we use the elements and principals of design to get us started? I want to say again that these are tools, not rules. Many successful artists create without thinking about these things. For me, the important thing is to recognize the elements in my everyday life and *see* like an artist. Using the principals of design, the elements can be added to make an artwork really sing. Like the color wheel, I often refer to the elements and principals when something is just not working. They are a benevolent guide. We can go astray as much as we want, but the elements and principals are always there to get us back on track.

MATERIALS

Now to the fun part! I have a philosophy about materials that I mostly stick to. I buy the best materials I can comfortably afford. I heard once that good tools aren't cheap and cheap tools aren't good. I think this applies to materials we use in the color, layer, stitch process as well. I don't advocate going into debt or spending more on materials than you can comfortably afford. I do advocate buying fewer numbers of better materials. Higher-quality pens, markers, and paints have more pigment, last longer, and won't be frustrating to use.

Life is full of choices, and here's a big one: Do you buy one of every color or do you buy a few colors and make do with what you have? *There is no correct answer.* Both approaches are perfectly acceptable. I personally am a buy-one-of-every-color collector. I generally use the paint right out of the bottle, and I have this irrational fear that the color I don't buy will be the exact one I need at some point.

Throughout the book, I will pose several "to be, or not to be" questions. The first is "To be or not to be formulated for use on fabric?" I am frequently asked what kind of paint I use. I use materials formulated for fabric, but not exclusively. Materials formulated for use on fabric have been tested for permanence and lightfastness on fabric. These materials are less likely to change the hand of the fabric, but some will still stiffen up when dry. When I am using a product *not* formulated for fabric, I always run a little test first. Is the product permanent when heat set? This means that if I heat set it and then go back with water, the pigment doesn't move. This is important not because I plan on washing my art quilts but because I might add layers that would cause the pigment to move if it weren't permanent after heat setting. I also don't want pigment on my drop cloth to migrate back onto my piece. Regardless of directions, I *heat set everything*. This will be an annoying reminder found throughout the book.

A few more words about permanence. I don't generally wash my quilted paintings, so colorfastness in the wash is less of a concern than it would be for a functional quilt. That said, I have had to wash quilted paintings, and it's nice to know I can with the assurance that the painting won't go away by doing so. Some products are permanent on fabric as soon as they have dried. I still heat set everything. I don't want something to bleed or migrate and surprise me. However, remember that if that happens, and it's likely that it will happen at some point, you can view it as an "embrace the blob" moment.

My goal is creative play and because of that, I don't stress about paint and the like being where I don't want it to be. I prefer to feel like I have a little control over the process, and heat setting is a great way to insure this as much as is possible. Another way to avoid unwanted surprises is to *test everything* before you use it on your painting. I have been surprised by products. Most watercolor products are not permanent even when heat set. It can be heartbreaking to find a brilliant color on your drop cloth finding its way up into a painting. My best advice is to not be heartbroken but embrace the blob and remember that sometimes "mistakes" make the best elements in a painting.

FABRIC

A word about fabric: To be prepared for dye (PFD) or not prepared for dye? That is the question. What is *PFD fabric*? It simply means that no sizing or other products have been added to the fabric. If we were using dye (we're not; we're using paint), we would need to have fabric free of any chemicals in order to facilitate the chemical reaction required with dye. Paint does not require a chemical reaction, so PFD fabric is not necessary. I use PFD because that is what I was taught to use. I continue to use Kona Cotton PFD because I like the hand and the weave. It is soft and takes paint well.

Any fabric can be used, and I have seen some lovely paintings on inexpensive unbleached muslin. Sometimes the drop cloth is mistaken for the painting fabric. I have also seen some amazing paintings on silk. Cotton is my preference, as the irresistible hand of silk is changed by most products, even "silk" paint. I just prefer quilting-weight cotton fabric. I learned years ago that a product's reaction on fabric has a great deal to do with the fabric—sometimes as much as or more than the product itself. If you want to experiment, take a small piece of any fabric and make a little test sheet to see how your products work on that fabric. I notice pigments bleed mostly with markers and paint. You will get a good feel for the fabric you prefer pretty quickly with a few tests.

BRUSHES

Let's talk brushes. A good paintbrush is really a thing of beauty. They can also be surprisingly expensive. I use cheap brushes. That way I can comfortably have a variety and choose the perfect size, shape, and stiffness. I have found that if a cheap brush is well cared for, I can get a pretty good life out of it. Additionally, I like to scrub with my brushes, and this more quickly compromises the bristles of any brush, regardless of cost or quality.

I prefer bristle brushes and Taklon brushes. I most often use flat or bright brushes, but you may find you prefer other shapes like round. I also like to use bristle stencil brushes, which generally have short, stiff round brush heads. No matter what brush you choose, taking good care of the brush will increase its lifespan. I use The Masters Brush Cleaner and Preserver (by General Pencil Company, Inc.). It gets all types of paint out of brushes and has the added benefit of conditioning the bristles a bit. The cakes last forever, and I find them to be easy to use. I always use tepid water to wash my brushes. Hot water will damage the glue on the ferrule, the part of the brush that holds the bristles on the handle. *Never, ever leave your brush bristle down in your water.* This is the easiest and fastest way to ruin any paintbrush, cheap or expensive. Not only does soaking in water damage the glue on the ferrule but soaking can also curl the bristles of the brush, and it is almost impossible to reshape them. Bristles can be a disadvantage when using very stiff brushes. They sometimes come out, even with fairly new and high-quality brushes. I'm sure my habit of scrubbing the brush is part of the problem. This is another reason I don't break the bank on paintbrushes. I like to scrub, I don't mind picking a bristle off the painting every now and then, and my heart doesn't break when bristle picking becomes too frequent and I toss the brush in the bin. I suggest you start with affordable (cheap) brushes. You will quickly find your favorite stiffness, bristles, shape, and size. Then you can decide if you want to go the cheap route or the expensive fine art route.

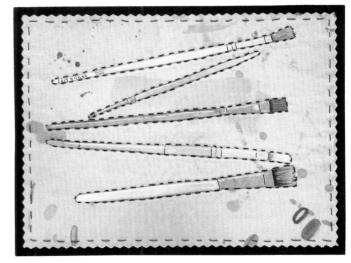

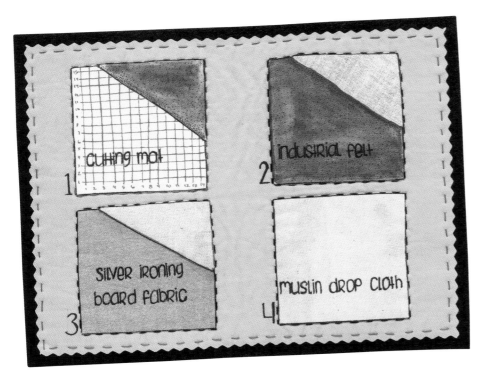

THE SETUP

Now let's talk about setup. I have toyed with many different ways to set up my work surface and have landed on one I really like. I paint and heat set right on my large cutting table, mat and all. I know—gasp. I have a Big-Mat rotary cutting surface on my table, and I don't want to remove it, roll it up, and find a place to keep it while I'm painting. I use 3 layers to protect the cutting mat when I paint. I start with thick industrial felt. Mine is very thick, almost ½″. I cover the felt with silver ironing board fabric (that's really what they call it). I then use a muslin drop cloth over the silver fabric.

THE IRON

The iron I use to flirt with disaster on my cutting mat is a dry iron. It has a smooth soleplate free of steam holes, gets very hot, is heavy, and doesn't have an auto-off function. As some of us have spent hundreds of dollars on irons, this affords

some assurance that you won't be cleaning paint out of the steam holes on your expensive tank iron. This little iron is affordable but sometimes hard to find. I can almost always find it on Amazon but have had to look at some of those websites that sell "old-fashioned" products. Except for the dazzling red color, I like how old-fashioned it looks. It reminds me of the iron and sprinkle bottle my Bunkie used when she ironed my grandpa's shirts on the back porch.

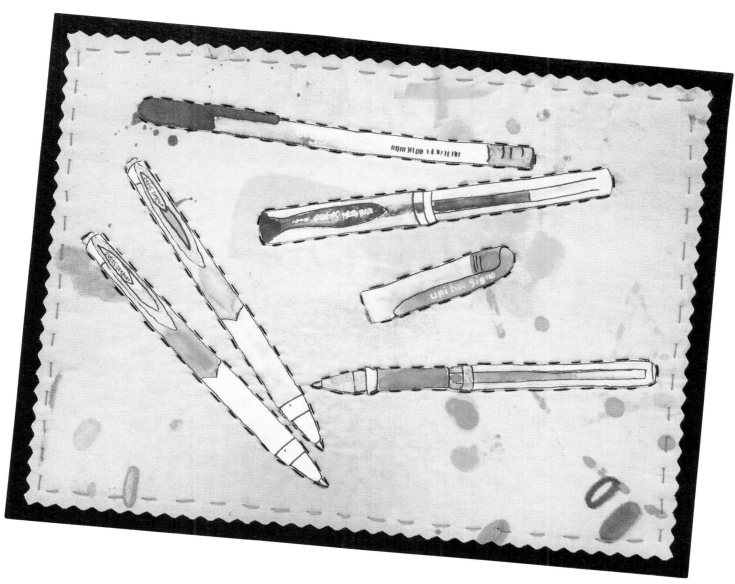

PENS

Now on to the good stuff. Let's start with pens. I will talk more in depth about how to use all these products in the next several chapters. This is a quick overview of what I use and why I use the products I do. I use a gel roller pen. Not all gel roller pens are created equal. If you use something I haven't listed, be *sure* to test it for permanence. Even pens that are permanent on paper can be fickle on fabric. My all-time favorite pen was the Pentel Gel Roller for Fabric pen. Of course, it has been discontinued, but I can still sometimes find them. What I use now are the Sakura Gelly Roll pens and any of the uni-ball Signo pens. Both are permanent on fabric (*heat set, heat set, heat set!*) and move pretty nicely across the tooth of the fabric. They both come in various sizes and colors. I like the 1.0mm or bold size, as I like my lines to be strong. The uni-ball Signo's white and metallic colors will not disappear on fabric and are lovely for bright accents on top of paints and markers.

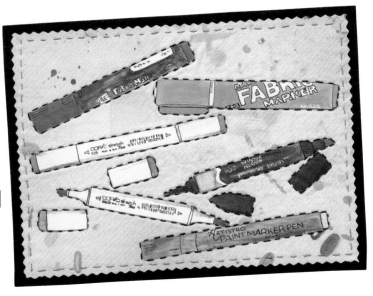

MARKERS

I like to use markers on fabric; they are fun and easy to use. Markers are a little easier to control than liquid paint, but they are not great for filling in large areas. There are several types of markers. The first are permanent or alcohol-based markers like Sharpie. This type of marker cannot be moved with water but is often alcohol soluble. Different types may *not* be permanent after heat setting, so test first if you venture into new types of markers. A good-quality permanent maker can be blended and will be a joy to use.

Copic *Sketch* markers are truly lovely. Although they are not formulated for fabric, they are a great addition to any fiber artist's toolbox. They are expensive fine art markers that come in a huge variety of colors, have dual tips, and are refillable. They have a brush end and a fine bullet end so you can do a lot of different things with one marker. These markers blend beautifully. The fact that they can be easily refilled, and the tips can be easily replaced, makes me happy. These markers do tend to bleed a bit on fabric. This is one product that I don't own in every color … I'm working on it though! They are juicy, truly high quality, and worth the investment. Also, they can be easily used on other surfaces, like paper. Don't be fooled by look-alike wannabe markers. They are just not the same.

Winsor & Newton Promarkers (formerly Letraset) are another high-quality fine art marker brand that works beautifully on fabric. They are a dual tipped with a chisel and bullet, and are really nice markers. They are also expensive and cannot be refilled. I have the Promarkers in those special colors that I can't find in other brands. They are permanent on fabric when heat set.

FabricMate DYE Ink Markers (by Yasutomo) are, obviously, formulated for fabric. They have a chisel tip, are juicy, and last a long time. They are available in a variety of colors, are easy to use, and can be blended. I appreciate the durability of the chisel tip on these markers. FabricMate markers are permanent when heat set.

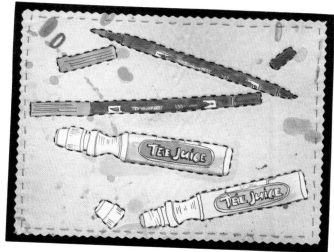

Marvy Fabric Markers (by Uchida of America) are big, juicy broad-tipped markers that are really fun to use. They have a fairly limited color palette, but the colors available are good. These markers last a long time, have a durable tip, and are permanent when heat set.

Tee Juice markers (by Jacquard Products) are formulated for fabric. They come in three different sizes, but I only use the broad-tip markers that look like bingo daubers. In my dry climate, the other sizes don't seem to stay juicy. The broad-tip markers are a great way to add a lot of color with decent control. It is also really fun to make dots with these paint-filled markers. They come in a limited color palette, are affordable, are really fun to use, and are permanent when heat set.

TEMPERA AND PIGMENT STICKS

I love little inexpensive solid tempera paints! Although they are not formulated for fabric, they work very well. They look like little lipsticks, although I haven't tried them as such. They are made for use by kids, they are very affordable, and they come in good colors. I like the tempera paint sticks from Shuttle Art; Kwik Stix (by The Pencil Grip) or Playcolor (by Jack Richeson & Co., Inc.) are also good affordable options. They are fun to use, provide a bit of almost opaque coverage, and are permanent when heat set.

Similar to the solid tempera paints are the Faber-Castell Gelatos. Unlike the solid temperas, they are very soft and creamy, and are also similar to lipsticks. They have a pretty good selection of colors and are affordable. They give beautiful soft color and are really fun to use. They move with water and aloe gel, glide across the fabric, and are permanent when heat set.

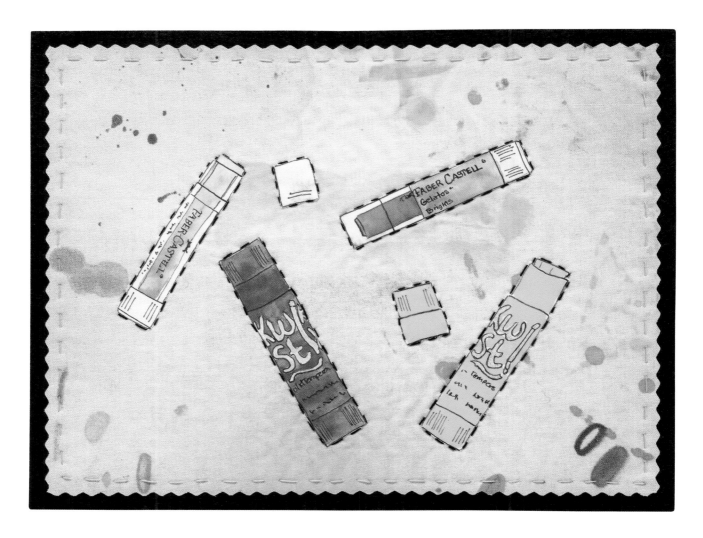

TEXTILE OR FABRIC PAINTS

I have used a lot of different paints formulated for fabric. They are all very similar
to one another. I've landed on PRO Silk & Fabric Paint (by PRO Chemical & Dye).
This paint is very thin, about the consistency of skim milk. It comes in an amazing
assortment of colors, is highly pigmented, and is easy to use. PRO Chemical & Dye
also makes a wonderful pearlescent paint, a thicker transparent textile paint (about the
consistency of sour cream), and an opaque paint. I recommend all of these paint products. That said, any fabric paint you already own or would like to try will work. I use
these paints straight out of the bottle. I'll show you later how to add aloe gel to the silk
& fabric paints to thicken them up a bit. All of the PRO Chemical & Dye paints are
permanent when heat set. Montana
Empty Crushers (by Montana-Cans)
are a great way to use silk paints. You
can fill these empty markers with any
liquid paint you like to use, and make
your own custom "bingo daubers."

I have also used a lot of materials
from Jacquard Products. I especially
like their Neopaque and Lumiere
paints. The Lumiere paints are
metallic and have a kind of magical
color-halo effect. I put these paints in
little needle-tip applicator bottles for
making beautiful lines. These paints
are permanent when heat set.

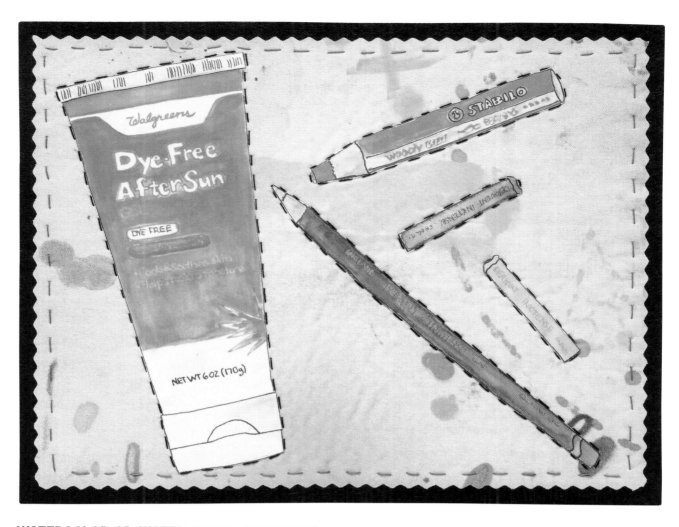

WATERCOLOR OR WATER-BASED PRODUCTS

As for water-based or watercolor pencils, beware. Not all are created equal. Some are true watercolor paints and will, therefore, never be permanent without adding some kind of medium to them. For a "watercolor" pencil that is permanent, my very favorite are Derwent Inktense Pencils and Blocks. They work like a watercolor pencil, but the binder is ink, so as soon as it is released with water or aloe, the pigment becomes permanent when heat set.

I also like STABILO Woody 3 in 1 watercolor pencils. They are really big and fat like crayons. They are made for kids, very affordable, and fun to use. Like the Inktense Pencils, they must be released with water or aloe in order to be permanent when heat set.

Both the Inktense pencils and blocks and the Woody 3 in 1 pencils must be released and *heat set* in order to be permanent. The obvious way to release them is to use water; that works great. What works even better is inexpensive aloe gel from the sunscreen aisle. I always get the dye-free version. I love using aloe gel because it doesn't bleed and gives me tremendous control. I've tried more expensive textile mediums and I don't like the effect as well. The mediums add a bit of acrylic to the fabric and change the hand of the fabric ever so slightly. I mentioned earlier that I sometimes use aloe gel to give a little more body to the very thin silk and fabric paints. Several companies make products, like colorless extenders and other mediums, but the aloe gel is inexpensive, doesn't change the hand of the fabric at all, and contains no acrylic, so clean up is a snap. Aloe can be used to move any water-based product.

OIL PAINT

One of my favorite products to use on fabric is oil sticks. Shiva Artist's PaintStiks (by Jack Richeson & Co., Inc.) are formulated for use on fabric. They are oil paint in a great big crayon form. You can use them directly on the fabric like a crayon or use a brush to apply them. They lay down beautiful color, blend marvelously, and add a lovely element to the painting. R&F Pigment Sticks are more expensive and softer than the Shiva PaintStiks. Formulated for fine artists, these paints are buttery soft, come in amazing colors, and are truly delicious. One of my favorite aspects of both types of paint is the linseed-oil smell. They make me feel like a "real artist" when I use them. They need to be allowed to dry completely, and then they need to be heat set. That brings me to one of the downsides of using oil paints. As you might imagine, oils need longer drying time. Shiva PaintStiks dry faster than R&F Pigment Sticks, but depending on humidity and the amount of paint, both can take several days to dry even after being heat set. This isn't a big deal to me; however, I have to remember to give them time so the painting doesn't become a mess.

I use Turpenoid Natural (by Martin F. Weber Co.) as a solvent with oil paints. It is a natural solvent that is nonflammable and nontoxic, has a pleasant smell, and is easily rinsed out with water. It also serves as a brush conditioner. I have used Turpenoid Natural as a medium to move and blend oil paint on paintings as well. The first time I did this, I was disappointed by the "shadow" it produced around the paint. I have since decided I like that effect, and now I do it on purpose.

I AM A MATERIAL GIRL

Whether you are a buy-one-of-every-color collector or a buy-a-few-colors collector, don't limit yourself to the products I use. There are a lot of products formulated for use on fabric. Many of them can be easily found in the big-box craft stores. Test everything before you use it on your next masterpiece. I've listed my favorites, but this list is nowhere near exhaustive. Dig into the art and craft supplies you already own, and give them a try! I know fantastic textile artists that use acrylic paints not formulated for fabric with great success without using textile medium. Give yourself permission to play and explore. You will soon discover your favorites.

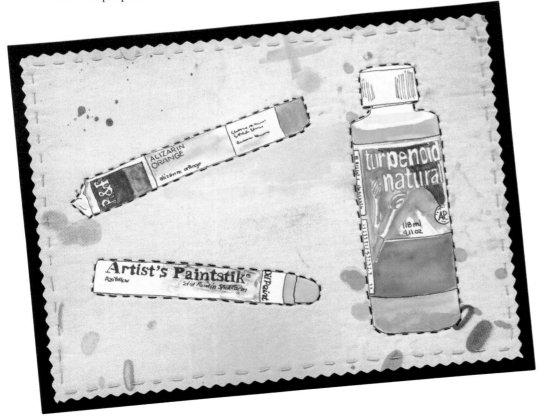

WHAT I DO

T he following chapters introduce how I add color to a painting. I first learned to paint on fabric from Susan Shie at Turtle Moon Studios. Not only does Susan make wonderful and thought-provoking art but she is also a delightful teacher and person. When I asked her, "How will I avoid making a cheap Susan Shie imitation?" she patted me on my cheek and replied, "Don't worry, Baby Tiger." It took me several years and several classes with Susan to embrace *my* artwork and *my* hand. I no longer worry about copying or being copied because unless you're an international art forger, it's impossible to make an exact copy. That said, if you ever copy someone else's work, be sure to give credit. My rule of thumb is that I would never sell anything that I've copied. If I use others' art as inspiration, I will say, "after Klimt," for example, to give credit to the original artist. Human beings learn by copying; just spend a few moments watching an infant. Many of the old masters learned by copying, but the paintings were always credited to the original artist, not the apprentice.

I have been painting on fabric for about fifteen years now. What I know about it comes from a lot of experimenting and taking classes from Susan Shie and Velda Newman, two fabulous and very different artists. Their art looks different, and they have different approaches to painting on fabric. I have taken what I learned and then experimented and played with many different products and techniques. What I'm sharing in this book is *my* way of painting and making marks on fabric. There are as many ways to do this as there are people painting on fabric. What follows is what I've learned through trial and error, with a generous measure of error. I encourage you to do your own experiments. You'll soon learn which materials you like and which materials you'll donate to a local art program.

A BIRD'S-EYE VIEW OF THE PROCESS

I always begin by *tearing* a piece of PFD (prepared for dye) Kona Cotton. I like the unfinished edges and the ease of tearing the fabric. This technique is all about creative freedom, and tearing the fabric at the beginning is a great way to set the attitude. That said, if that drives you crazy then you should use a ruler and a rotary cutter. There is no wrong way to do this. I'll say it again: This book and its techniques are all about the process. The fun (and creative growth) is in the doing. If you are thrilled with your outcome, that's icing on the cake. If you don't like it, cut it up!

After I've torn the fabric to the size I want, I divide the blank space using a pen (there will be more about pens in the next chapter, Pens, page 55). I work right on my cutting table, heat setting and all. I lay a piece of industrial felt down on my cutting surface, cover that with silver ironing board fabric, lay down a drop cloth, and go to work. When I first began, I used a double layer of cotton batting under the silver ironing board fabric, and that works well, too. The industrial felt is squishier than the double layer of batting. I don't mind that, but if you fall in love with this process, you may want to consider your preferences. My iron sometimes bubbles my Big-Mat cutting mat, and if that happens, I just go over that area again with the iron and hold it flat until it cools off.

Layer industrial felt over the cutting mat.

Layer silver ironing cloth and then a drop cloth.

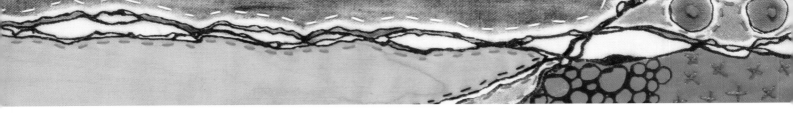

I like to set it up this way because I can heat set a painting without moving it to the ironing board, I don't get paint on my ironing board, and I heat set the drop cloth at the same time as I'm heat setting the painting.

A few words about heat setting—I always create a sandwich with my painting: drop cloth under the painting and drop cloth over the painting. This protects both the painting from the iron and the iron from the painting.

Also, *iron—do not press*. We are trained as quilters to press (an up-and-down motion with the iron). In this process, keep the iron moving. It's very easy to burn the image of an iron into wet paint, and I have yet to discover how to conceal that. It always, always looks like an iron.

Always use a smooth cotton pressing cloth, as the texture from the pressing cloth will be immediately transferred to the painting. (Unless you want the texture from the pressing cloth, which might be really cool—this is just another example of how you can't do this wrong!) Experiment, play, enjoy. Reacquaint yourself with that little child who delighted in creativity. I know he or she is in there.

Sometimes I start with a color palette in mind; sometimes I don't. I rarely stick to the palette I've started with in any case. I use the color wheel when I want something to pop or to recede. Remember that the color wheel, *any* color wheel, is a tool, not a rule.

The most important thing you can take away from this book is to enjoy what you're doing, embrace the blob (it's very likely you'll have several to embrace), and reconnect to your unique creativity.

The hardest part of starting anything is starting. The hardest thing about starting a quilted painting is staring at a pristine piece of white fabric. Start *small*. Like fat quarter, or smaller still. This little piece is only 9″ × 11″.

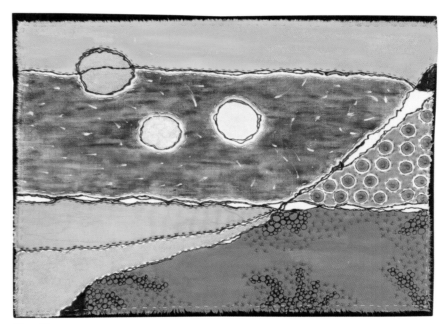

Three Moons

There's nothing wrong with making a few *tiny* pieces to get the feel of the material. Here are some little prayer flag–size paintings. These tiny ones are some of my favorites. Each tiny piece is about 4″ × 9″.

Flag One

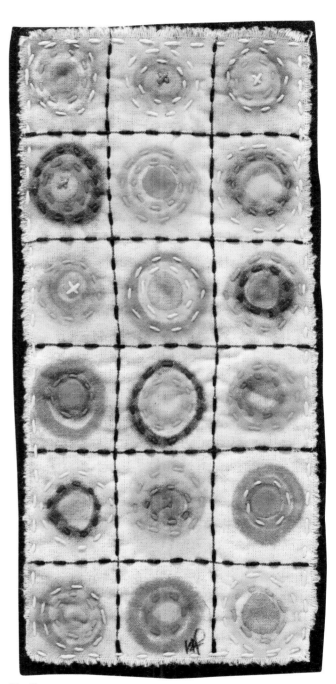

Flag Two

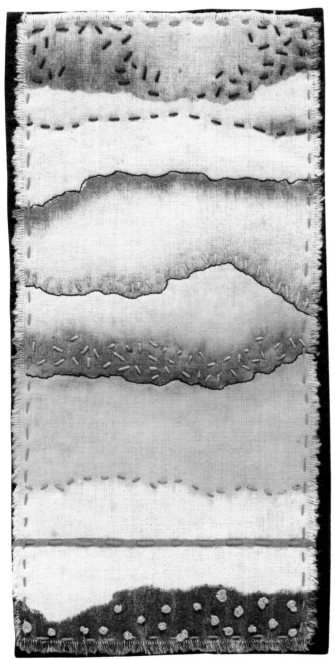

Flag Three

Flag Four

No matter what the size, you will still be staring at a blank sheet of white fabric. I had to get over feeling like fabric was more precious than paper. I also had to remind myself that if it's only a small piece of even the finest white cotton fabric, it can be replaced for only a few dollars, even less if you start tiny.

That said, the logical thing to do is to divide the blank piece of white fabric into smaller sections. Once the pen hits the fabric for the first time and it bobbles and creates a "mistake," you'll be fine. This process is not about perfection. It's about the fun we can have engaging in childlike creative play. We all love playing with fabric and colors, so why not make your own fabric with the colors you love? Also, remember to embrace the blob.

YOU ARE HERE (OR HOW TO GET WHERE YOU WANT TO GO)

If you are trying to orient yourself on any type of map, you need to know where you are. Picture the map in the mall that has the iconic "you are here" with an arrow pointing to the spot where you stand. Or picture the little blue dot that moves on your digital map as you navigate your travels. Well, you are here. You are staring at a pristine piece of white fabric.

To find directions on any kind of map, you need to know where you are going. Your blue dot is stationary because you have no idea in which direction to start. What follows are some common tried-and-true composition maps that you can use. Again, these composition maps are tools, not rules. Use them if you'd like or ignore them if you prefer. Combine them and play with them if that sounds fun. These are your starting points with an arrow showing which direction you might travel. Whichever way you venture, remember this is fun. Embrace the blob, and if you don't like it in the end, you can cut it up!

Framing (Self-Portrait in Rome)

Framing is the presentation of an object within a frame. A frame can make an image more pleasing to the viewer as well as keep the viewer focused on the objects within the frame. A frame can add interest to a painting, especially when the frame is thematically related to the object being framed.

Self-Portrait Rome

Horizontal Line (The Gloaming)

A horizontal line, sometimes called a *horizon line*, is a great way get started with a painting. It implies grounded-ness and stability. The horizon line can be placed at approximately a division of thirds (this always works) or bisecting the painting (this is harder to make work).

The Gloaming is entirely paint. I started with the bold turquoise line and used a sponge to apply Dye-Na-Flow paint (by Jacquard Products).

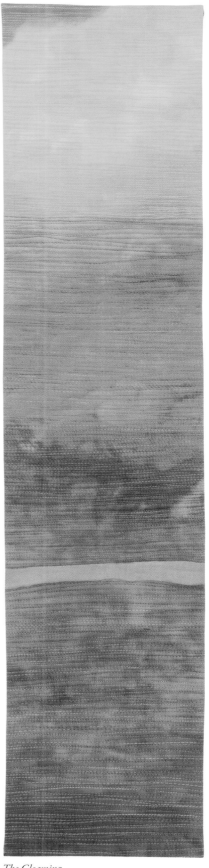

The Gloaming

Don't Tell Me It's Easier Alone
Photo by Katie Fowler

Rule of Thirds (Don't Tell Me It's Easier Alone)

Sometimes referred to as the *golden section* or the *divine ratio*, the rule of thirds states that the focal point of a composition should fall at the intersection of two lines. I sometimes use actual lines to start a painting using the rule of thirds. I rarely measure and usually eyeball it. Beware: Golden ratios, Fibonacci numbers, and fractals are a really fun rabbit hole for starting art projects.

Don't Tell Me It's Easier Alone is one of the early wholecloth paintings I did. The messy corner represents the things we keep secret. Life is much easier when we share our vulnerabilities and don't hide ourselves from others.

Rule of Odds (Helios Trebled)

If you have more than two of any element, you should have an odd number. Odd numbers provide more interest and tension than even numbers.

Helios Trebeled is a little piece done purely for the fun of putting marks on fabric.

Helios Trebled

Asilomar Cilantro

Radial Design (Asilomar Cilantro)

Radial design is most often found in mandalas (the word *mandala* means "circle" in Sanskrit). It starts at the center and grows outward from there. It usually, but not always, uses formal symmetry.

Asilomar Cilantro was made in an Empty Spools class with Barbara Olsen. It is appliqué using her unique method.

Once in a While

Grid (Once in a While)

Familiar to quilters as the basis for most traditional quilt-block patterns, the grid in art quilts can be formal or informal. We can use an actual grid pattern, complete with measured lines and straight edges, or we can hint at a grid pattern.

Once in a While is an experiment to see what I could do with a grid and concentric circles. I colored it using markers and shaded it with oil sticks.

Line (Contradictions)

Using line as a starting point in a painting is a great way to begin. I like to think of letters as a starting point for this structure. A line can be an O, C, S, or H shape to get you started. It can also be an organic line that doesn't represent any letter.

I started *Contradictions* with one line in black and built the painting around that line. The grid came later.

Contradictions

Overall Patterning (Chockablock)

If you use the same, similar, or related shapes in a seemingly random way, you have used overall patterning. That may be what you want. Placing shapes at interesting intervals is the key here. A slight variation in size and color can make this successful.

Chockablock is appliquéd bricks in many different fabrics.

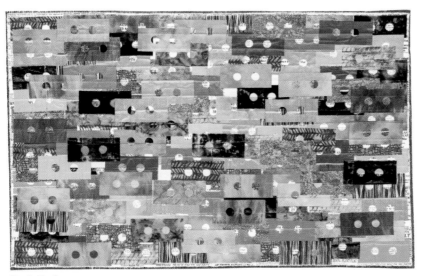

Chockablock

A FINAL WORD ABOUT MAPS

The important thing to remember about the composition maps is that they are just suggestions. Maps don't decide where we are going; they suggest ways to get there. I hardly ever start out with a complete composition in my mind. In fact, I'm not sure I've ever done that. These suggestions are starting points from which you can vary your journey in whatever way suits your fancy. Don't forget to embrace the blob.

PENS

A WORD ABOUT CREATIVITY

Getting started is often the hardest part of the creative process. This is true for many different activities. The hardest part of any walk is walking out the door. That said, how do you get started? I have two never-fail tips for you. First, start small. Very small. Fat quarter small. Second, let go of any expectations. Remember: If you aren't happy with the outcome, cut it up!

THE PEN CHECK

If you use a pen different from what I've tested, it's a good idea to run a little test of your own. Heat set the pen, put other materials over it, heat set, and wash it. Make sure the pen will play nicely with others.

PREPARING THE FABRIC

When I start any painting, I decide about how big I want it to be. I always eyeball it. I'm not big on measuring. Then I tear the fabric. I like the organic fringy edge and the wonky not quite square that gives me. Plus, it's really fun to tear fabric! If you prefer, use a ruler and a rotary cutter. There really aren't any rules.

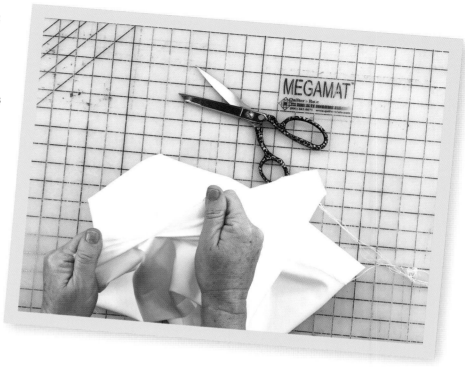

I always run a lint roller and an iron over the fabric to give myself a nice surface.

STARING AT A PIECE OF WHITE FABRIC

Now what? You have a piece of pristine white fabric. This is the scary part, and you have to jump in. I almost always start by dividing the space into smaller spaces using a pen. In this case, I'm using a uni-ball Signo pen.

I have a few go-to compositions that I really like. The three circles use the Rule of Odds composition map and this diagonal division sort of references the rule of thirds. I can almost guarantee you that your pen will skip and bobble. To (mostly) avoid this, move the pen slowly and hold the fabric tight behind the pen.

Note: Stabilizing the Fabric
I don't stabilize my fabric when I paint. Some like to use freezer paper; that's a personal choice. If you choose to stabilize the fabric, iron some freezer paper (shiny side to the fabric) on the back of your fabric.

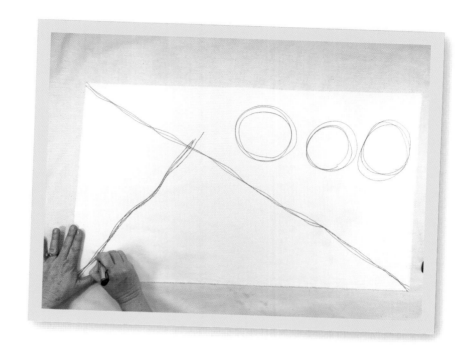

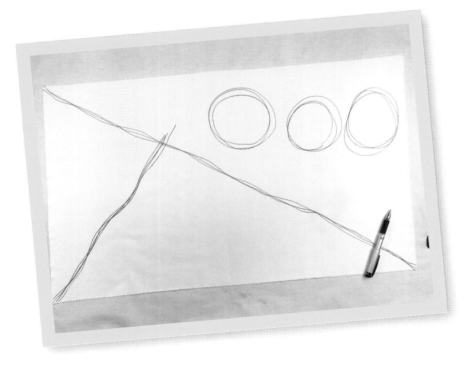

I go back to the pen often during the painting process. I always go over the initial line to make it darker and bolder. It doesn't bother me when the pen veers off the original line. I like the variation it gives to the line width. It makes it look cool!

MORE WAYS TO START

Here are a few other ideas to get you started. These haven't become paintings yet. If I don't like the pen marks, I keep the fabric as a tester or revisit it later and maybe take it further.

A WORD ABOUT CREATIVITY

Mistakes happen—they just do. At least they always happen for me. I like to think of them the way the famous PBS painter Bob Ross did, as "happy little accidents." Markers bleed, some more than others. Just accept it and move on. Like they say, "If it looks good galloping by on a horse …" Others will not look at your quilts with anything like the critical eye you do.

COLORING FOR PROFESSIONALS

I like to call this layer of adding color "coloring for professionals." One of the most important parts of coloring for professionals is holding your tongue just right. I almost always have chapped lips, and it's because I use my tongue to make art quilts. This is a physical manifestation of hyper focus, so I just accept it and buy more lip balm.

MARKERS FOR MARK-MAKING

There are several different types of markers I like to use. Any of the permanent markers listed in Markers (page 42) are great to use. I choose which marker to use by the size of the tip and the range of colors. I wish I could afford to have every color in the Copic and Windsor & Newton markers, but I can't. Both markers have a dual tip, so they are good for filling in tiny spaces, small spaces, and creating fine lines. The downside of these markers is they tend to bleed a little bit. The Marvy Fabric Markers and FabricMate markers don't bleed much if at all.

I like to start by filling in a few little spaces and getting my color scheme started. Here I'm using a Copic marker.

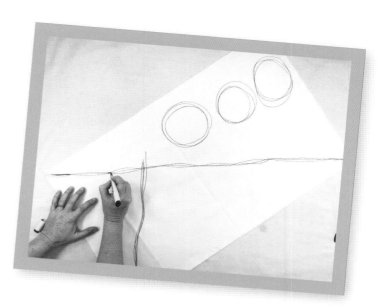

BIG CHUNKY MARKERS (LIKE BINGO DAUBERS)

When I want to fill in a larger space or create exciting little dots, I use Tee Juice markers or my Montana Crusher markers filled with PRO Silk & Fabric Paints. Both types of markers usually need a *gentle* squeeze to get the paint flowing through the tip. They can be a bit unpredictable at times, so don't forget to embrace the blob.

I start with the lightest color and then add sequentially darker colors.

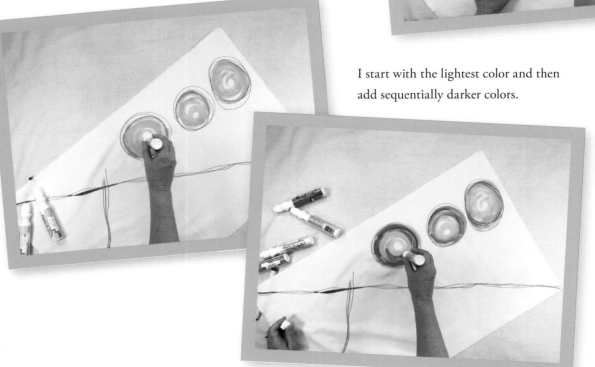

These blend beautifully. I usually go back over the whole thing with the lightest yellow just to blend them a little more. Don't worry about color on the tips of the lighter markers. Give them a swipe on your drop cloth.

I love filling in the little spaces my wonky lines leave!

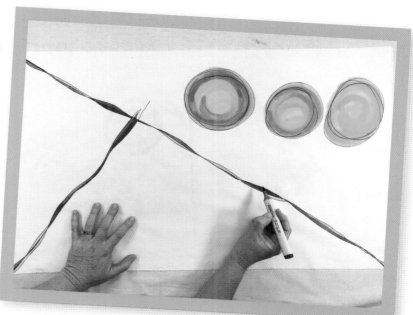

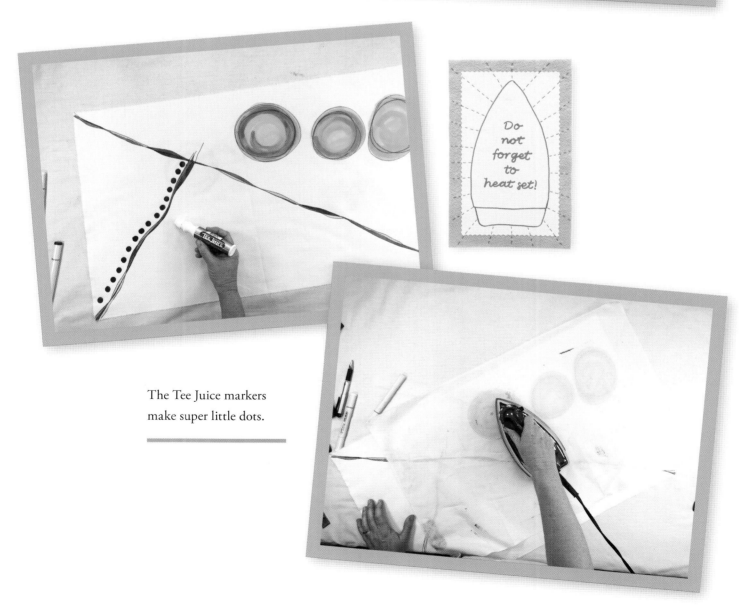

The Tee Juice markers make super little dots.

Do not forget to heat set!

IT'S LIKE A DANCE

I go back to pens and dance around with products. Here I'm outlining the green dots with a gold uni-ball Signo pen.

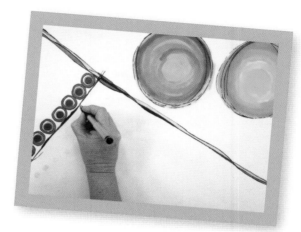

And now with a red marker.

I'll often go back in and make the black lines thicker and darker as I go along.

GOOD THINGS HAPPEN IN SMALL SPACES

I want to divide the space up even more. This is where the composition starts to take shape. I loosely determine a horizontal third (remember the rule of thirds?) and add a few more pen lines.

Color inspiration can come from many different places. This little thread nest kept showing up and the colors made me happy. I kept it on my table while I worked on this piece.

I hope you're having fun!

WATER-BASED PAINTS

A WORD ABOUT CREATIVITY

It is so important to allow yourself to be a beginner. This is hard for us as adults, especially if we pick things up easily. Your paint will most certainly drip, or bleed, or even spill. It's happened to me, and I've seen it happen to others. Take a deep breath. Remember you are doing this for fun. And for goodness' sake, *embrace the blob*!

HOW DO YOU DO (IT)

Are you a straight-out-of-the-bottle painter, or do you like to mix it up? I am generally a straight-out-of-the-bottle painter. That's why I'm a buy-every-color shopper! This isn't just because I like to have every color, although that's true—I do. I paint straight out of the bottle because I think it wastes less paint. I'm never sure how much paint I'll need, so I don't want to mix too much. Also, I don't want to under-mix and have to match the color I was using.

The paints we are using mix beautifully on the fabric, and this is true for all brands. I like the mottled look better than a whole field of a solid color anyway.

POPULATING THE FIELDS

I begin by adding a little bright blue-green
with a Montana Crusher marker filled
with Pro Silk & Fabric paint. This paint
has the consistency of skim milk.

Next, I add a contrasting color to the
blue. I paint a bit of a yellow-orange
tone in the adjacent triangle, this time
using the thicker transparent paint, the
consistency of hand lotion.

Now I add the complement to the yellow-
orange, blue-violet, and paint it around the
circles. By this time, I've named this piece
Europa and Her Sisters, so the circles are now
moons.

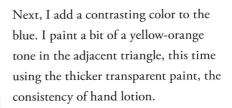

I use several different blue-violets from the
PROfab Transparent textile paint line. This
is an example of mixing colors on the fabric.

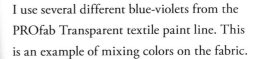

CHECK THIS OUT

Adding layers of interest is like a dance. I like to put checks in most things I paint; it's kind of my trademark. So, back to the black uni-ball Signo pen to draw in some checks. I don't want these to be perfect straight lines and uniform checks. I've done this so much that my muscle memory wants to make them straight and uniform. I have to concentrate on making them a bit wonky.

A red uni-ball Signo pen makes some bigger red checks in the bottom corner. A deep red Marvy Fabric Marker is speedier and less frustrating than a gel roller pen for filling in the checks.

I went back in around the moons with a yellow marker to fill the gaps between the moons and the background.

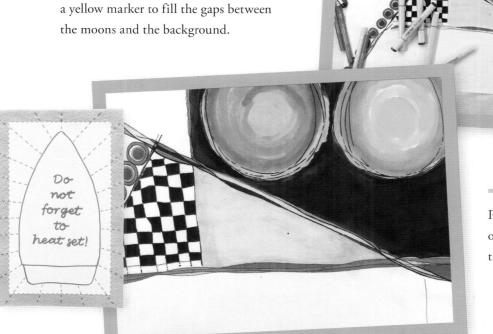

Do not forget to heat set!

Please notice the drips of violet on the yellow triangle. Drips happen!

TEMPERA CRAYONS
AND PIGMENT STICKS

A WORD ABOUT CREATIVITY

Creativity is hard. It's like pulling your
innermost self out and setting it on the table.
It's also one of the most wonderful and human
endeavors available. If you're stuck, it's creative
chaos; remember to stay for the cake! If you're
afraid you'll ruin it, it's likely one of the
creativity crushers or perfectionism speaking.
Figure out what is making you afraid, and
remember: no heads were chopped off by the
Queen of Hearts.

ARTISTIC TEMPERA-MENT

Tempera crayons and Gelato pigment sticks are delightful little sticks of color that look like lip balm. They are formulated for kids, so they are safe and nontoxic. They are a bit difficult to control for fine work, but for big, bold splashes of color, they are the bomb.

I've added an extra diagonal line to create another division of space and added some green dots with marker to the bright blue field.

I want to add some small-scale detail to the piece. Scale is one of the principals of design discussed in Composition and Design (page 34). Differing scales, like the different-size checks, add interest to a composition. I use the uni-ball Signo pen to draw some little bubbles and use light green tempera to fill in the middle of those little bubbles.

My little green dots are lost on the blue, so I added some bright green Gelato to give them a little more life.

WHAT'S MY LINE?

Next comes a bold bright-blue line across the entire composition made with a Gelato. It gives the illusion of a broken line, or perhaps the line goes under the checks and dots. I smoothed the line with a stiff stencil brush.

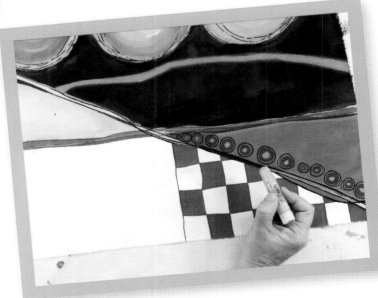

Another small area with bubbles and bright green balances out those bright colors. The bright green in the bubbles is tempera and Gelatos blended to make it more interesting and give it depth.

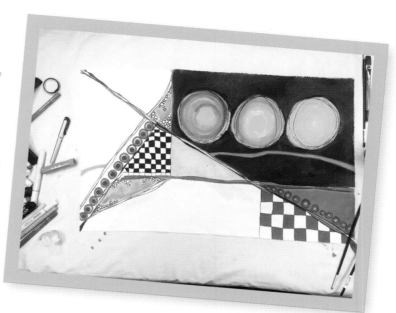

LET'S DANCE

I dance back to water-based paints, again using PROfab Transparent textile paint. I use two colors of green and several colors of blue. You can really see the mixing on fabric in the blue section. I just kind of pounce my brush to mix the colors on the fabric.

Do not forget to heat set!

OIL PAINT ON FABRIC

A WORD ABOUT CREATIVITY

What inspires you? Is it colors? Fabric? Maybe it's the artwork of others. There is no right or wrong when it comes to inspiration. Pay attention to what kinds of things get your creative juices flowing. I love music and stories. I often name my quilts after songs or parts of stories that I love. Notice your inspiration. Picasso said, "Inspiration exists, but it has to find you working."

THE GREAT RED SPOT

One of my favorite parts of the process is naming a quilt. I hardly ever start a project with a name in mind. Often the name, or an idea for a name, just comes to me as I'm working. This project reminds me of a piece I did years ago called *Three Moons*. That got me to thinking about Jupiter with its multiple moons. That's how I came up with the name *Europa and Her Sisters*. It isn't scientifically based but was the inspiration for how I used oil paints on this piece.

The large space in the bottom center of the piece is to become the surface of Jupiter with its iconic storm called The Great Red Spot. I used my imagination on the colors and tried to recreate the surface of Jupiter sitting below Europa and her sisters.

WHAT'S YOUR SCHTICK?

Oil sticks are simply oil paint in crayon form.
They are really delicious to use on fabric, the only
drawback being drying time. You can find more
on oil sticks in Oil Paint (page 46). What you
need to know is that oil sticks form a protective
skin when not in use. This skin is a thin coating
of dry paint that needs to be removed in order to
use the paint. I live in a very dry climate, and I
have to use an X-ACTO knife to remove the skin.

Simply and carefully shave the skin off
the end of the oil stick. Unfortunately, I
have not been able to find a use for these
beautiful cast offs except to keep them in
a mason jar. They won't melt and can't be
reconstituted in any way that I've been able
to discover… and believe me, I've tried.

Some brands allow the skin to be peeled.
This may work for all of them if you live in
a humid area.

LAY IT ON THICK

Use the oil sticks just like a giant
crayon. This part can get messy, so I
always change into a paint shirt. It's
really fun to run the soft oil stick across
the fabric and watch the color build.

Sometimes I use a little bit of Turpenoid on a brush to help the colors blend. This creates a little ghost or shadow around the paint. I really like this effect, but the first time it happened I had to remind myself of Bob Ross' "happy little accidents."

Paint can also be picked up on a brush directly from the oil stick. I always use stencil brushes with stiff bristles for this process. It's a really nice way to lay rich color on a painting in small amounts. This technique is great for shading.

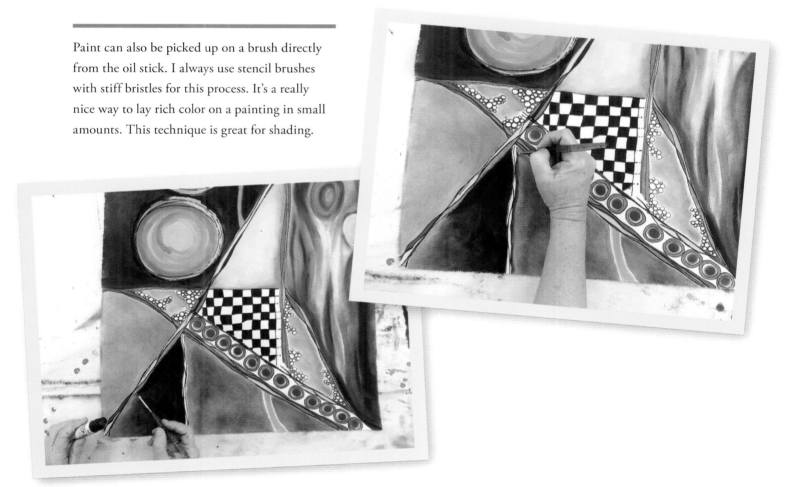

LET'S DANCE

I want to circle back to pens and add some stark white on either side of the bright blue line. This will make it stand out and add some depth.

Do not forget to heat set!

DERWENT INKTENSE AND STABILO WOODY PENCILS

A WORD ABOUT CREATIVITY

Almost always my pieces grow through a "teenager phase." They aren't quite turning out the way I thought they would. My kids take great umbrage with this reference, and for the record our kids turned out just fine. This is creative chaos. Don't stop. Don't give up on it. Keep going. By now you have several layers on the fabric, which, if the composition doesn't please you, will at least make interesting little mini masterpieces if you decide to cut it up. I am a recovering start over-er … don't do that to yourself. Just keep going.

SHADES OF COLOR

When a block of color looks too solid, or something needs a little pizzazz, Derwent Inktense or STABILO Woody 3 in 1 pencils are a great choice. You can find information on water-based products in Watercolor or Water-Based Products (page 45). Remember that not all watercolor pencils are permanent, so choose wisely.

The yellow-orange section needed a little life; I added this with an Inktense pencil and blended it with aloe gel.

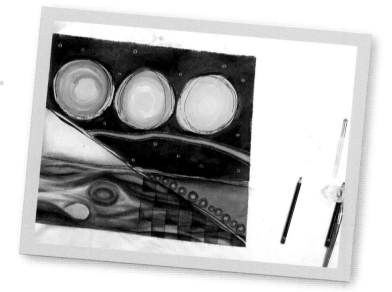

I did the same with the bright blue section.

I wanted to emphasize the large red checks I covered with oil paint, so I added a little red shading to the squares.

LET'S DANCE

I want a little more interest in the upper left corner. I use opaque India ink in a little spray bottle to give some texture to that area.

I also used a gold uni-ball Signo pen to draw little circles in the background behind the moon. Stars, maybe? I can see stitching little French knots in each circle.

LET'S TAKE A LOOK

Now it's time to hang it on my design wall and look at it for a few days. That's how I determine if it's finished. Notice its wonky shape. That's from tearing the fabric and my manipulation of the wet media I used on the painting. This usually doesn't bother me. See Now What? (page 110) for alternative solutions for the wonkiness.

Do not forget to heat set!

LESSONS

A WORD ABOUT CREATIVITY

The more you make, the more "good" stuff you make. For years, I marveled at my proficient fellows. They seem to crank out one good thing after another. I couldn't do this. Now I can. Why? Because of all the things I've already talked about. I laugh at the creativity crushers, I let perfectionism go, I (mostly) don't compare myself to others, I take care of my creative self, and I embrace creative chaos. I just do it!

SELF-PORTRAIT COPENHAGEN

I love to name my quilts, and the name usually comes to me partway through the process. Our daughter studied in Copenhagen her junior year in college. I got to go visit her for a mom/daughter week and we had such fun. While she was in class, I rode my rental bike all around the city and explored, went to art museums, and enjoyed charming little coffee shops. This is my self-portrait to remind me of that magical trip.

This little piece (20″ × 16″) is an example of using a frame as a composition map. I start with the frame and go from there. I'm not too worried about the lines being exactly straight. I go over the lines several times because I like to, but also because it makes the squiggles and baubles look purposeful.

I reference a photo of the famous NyHavn taken on that trip. I added myself on the bike in the sky as I wasn't actually able to fly over Copenhagen. I am not worrying about perspective and realism, as that would take all the fun out of it for me. Remember, there are no rules. So if you want to be more realistic, by all means do what thrills *you*.

The sky looks a bit empty, so I add a curious moon and paint her with PROfab Pearlescent Paint (by PRO Chemical & Dye). I leave parts of the moon unpainted to mimic the craters we see when we look at the real moon.

It always helps to move to something rather simple, so I color in the roofs using a variety of Copic markers. I want the roofs, which are all the same in reality, to have a little variation, so I mix the colors as I go.

Next, I color the windows with a gray Marvy Fabric Marker.

The window frames on the yellow building are black, so I use my uni-ball Signo pen for that.

You know the drill ... do not forget to heat set!

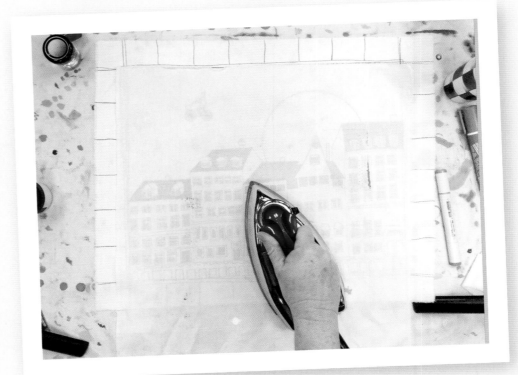

The pen and markers are heat set. I color the buildings using Derwent Inktense Pencils. They must be released, so I use aloe gel. I reference my photo for the building colors.

I use a variety of Copic markers, which blend and run into each other, to color the sky. I take advantage of the unpredictable properties of mixing the colors to mimic a dynamic cloudy sky.

I use a red uni-ball Signo pen to fill in parts of the frame.

Now I'm a bit stumped as to what I want to do with that frame. As I contemplate the frame, I notice the window frames are getting a bit lost in the colors, so I go back in with a white uni-ball Signo pen and "repaint" the windows. Much better.

I make the divisions in the frame a heavier black and add some folk art designs to give more color … red, of course. It's Denmark! I draw the designs with a red uni-ball Signo pen and use Derwent Inktense Pencils and Marvy Fabric Markers to color them in. I don't want them all exactly the same red.

For a look at the finished piece, see Machine Quilting (page 127).

DROUK LOVE

I use the horizontal-line composition map for this 25″ × 18″ piece. I just jump in with an oil stick and start the composition.

I pretty much hate this piece right now, but decide to practice what I preach and keep going. I can always cut it up, right?

I use a stiff stencil brush and a dab of Turpenoid Natural to blend some of the colors and soften the edges between colors.

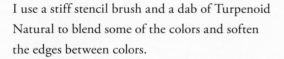

Not hating it quite as much now.

This piece is painted entirely with oil paints. I have to admit: When I use oil paints, I feel like a real artist. I love the smell of linseed oil. Also, I am usually covered in paint at the end of the day. For me, oils definitely require a paint shirt; an apron just won't do. Sometimes it's even on my face and in my hair!

For a look at the finished piece, see Machine Quilting (page 127).

ORCHARD LADDER

No clever name for this little piece. The circles started to look like trees to me, so I made them the colors of peaches, plums, and pears, imagining that the color of the fruit trees matched their fruit. Wouldn't that be a Dr. Seuss world?

Orchard Ladder demonstrates the rule of thirds/odds. I use both of these composition maps in this piece. I know it's not really thirds, but I never let that stop me. I just doodle a little with a uni-ball Signo pen and add some more elements to the piece. Some checks, of course. Three circles and a diagonal line.

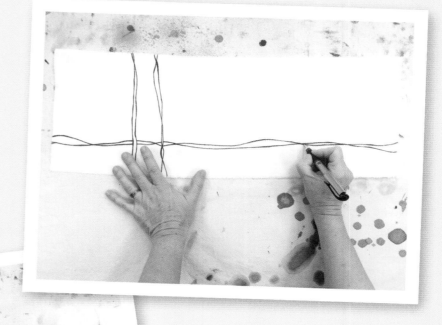

I want to make the lines heavier and blacker, so I go over them with the uni-ball Signo pen. I fill in the checks with the uni-ball Signo pen as well.

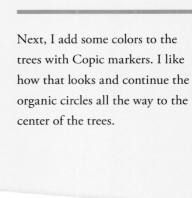

I add some dark green PRO Silk & Fabric Paint for the ground around the trees.

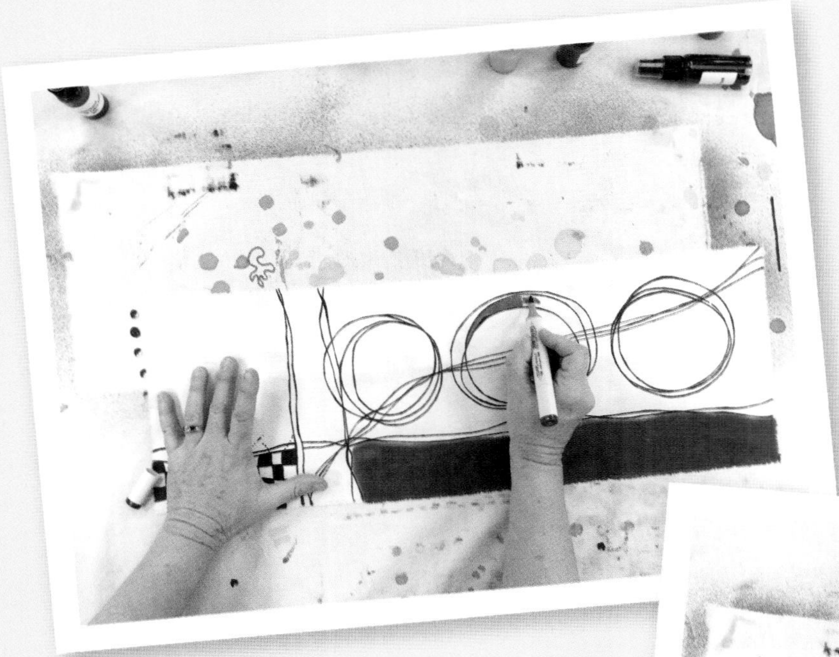

Next, I add some colors to the trees with Copic markers. I like how that looks and continue the organic circles all the way to the center of the trees.

I finish adding color to the trees and go over my pen lines with the uni-ball Signo again. I also spot a place for some more checks (sort of). I add a little stripe of sunshine with a yellow uni-ball Signo pen and go over it with a Marvy Fabric Marker.

I use two different light blue Copic markers to add color to the sky. I use STABILO Woody pencils for a halo effect around the trees.

Now it goes onto the design wall for some percolation about what comes next. I do not work start to finish on one piece. As you can see, I usually have several projects on the wall at the same time, especially when writing a book!

I add a little violet with a STABILO Woody pencil and blend it with aloe gel. I use Lumiere paint in a needle-tip applicator to add some tree trunks and few little red circles.

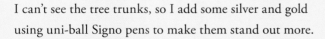

I can't see the tree trunks, so I add some silver and gold using uni-ball Signo pens to make them stand out more.

Working small like this is satisfying and really fun.

For a look at the finished piece, see Organic Hand Stitching (page 125).

IDUNN'S ORCHARD

Yes! You can! Idunn is the Norse goddess of spring, and she grows the apples that the gods eat to gain immortality. As I was adding color to this mandala, it just started looking like spring to me. After a brief dive into the internet to research spring, I found Idunn. All the little circles remind me of her apples.

I begin by tearing a piece of fabric as square as it will tear. I find the middle by folding and pressing on the diagonal twice and with the grain twice.

Pretty easy so far. Now I doodle using my fold lines as a guide. I do not worry about everything being exactly uniform. If I want that, I'll use a kaleidoscope program on the computer. Enjoy this—no stress! It will end up looking good. I promise.

I use what I have around the studio to keep me round. Here I am using a drafting template and embroidery hoops.

I just keep doodling, reminding myself that it doesn't matter if my doodles aren't uniform because it really doesn't matter.

Like Dori from the *Finding Nemo* movie says, "Just keep swimming; just keep swimming."

I made a boo-boo when I was working on the new circle. It doesn't matter! I make the circle a thick black line and just keep going.

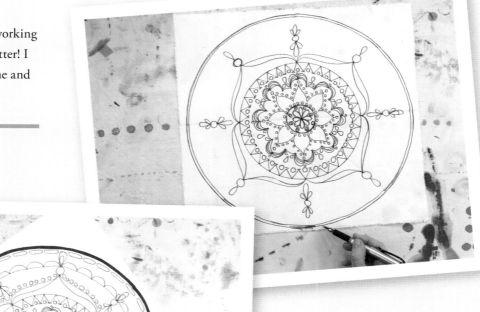

Now for the fun part. You will see how the imperfections really don't matter. In fact, I think they add to the organic nature of the mandala, especially when I start to add color.

I use Derwent Inktense
Pencils and aloe gel to begin.
The pencils come alive when
released with the aloe gel.
Yep, we're still heat setting!

I keep working until I think I need the stronger colors of the Marvy Fabric Markers. Mix it up to make it look the way you want. No rules, except heat setting!

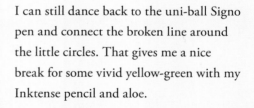

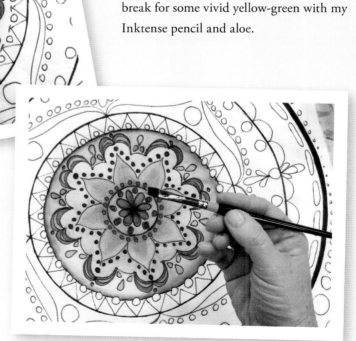

I can still dance back to the uni-ball Signo pen and connect the broken line around the little circles. That gives me a nice break for some vivid yellow-green with my Inktense pencil and aloe.

Here's a trick for using the beautiful and transparent PRO Silk & Fabric Paints in an intricate spot. Grab a tiny container and add a squirt of aloe. Pour a little paint in the container with the aloe and pour the extra back into the paint bottle. Mix well with your paintbrush and you will have a beautiful, transparent, and controllable paint to add to your piece.

I rarely let anything leave my worktable without checks or stripes of some kind. I use my black uni-ball Signo pen to add my signature.

For a look at the finished piece, see Machine Quilting (page 127).

KANDINSKY KOPIED

You may be familiar with the very famous circles by Wassily Kandinsky. His title for this piece is *Color Study, Squares with Concentric Circles*. I looked at Kandinsky's piece and made my own version. I certainly used the same layout that he used; however, I did not copy his colors. I didn't look again at his piece while I was painting this.

This is a good example of the grid composition map. Quilters seem to like grids. I know I love a good grid. I begin by folding the fabric to establish a rough idea of how I want the grid placed. In the spirit of a color study, I used my color wheel to choose PRO Silk & Fabric Paints in Montana Crusher markers.

Then I laid the markers out on the grid to establish how I wanted the colors placed.

Using the principles of color theory, I start painting. I think about complementary colors to provide contrast. Then I add the colors that I want. The colors bleed into each other, but that is what I want. The repetitive shapes provide unity while the colors provide contrast.

For a look at the finished piece, see Slice and Dice (page 113).

MAD HATTER'S LOVE LETTER

The name of this painting seems obvious to me. It is bright and chaotic and filled with hearts. It has to have something to do with the Mad Hatter.

Yes, you can do this, too! A line starts this whole thing. Just a simple little line. When using a line as your composition map, it can be as simple or as complicated as you want it to be. I draw this line with a black uni-ball Signo pen. I see a ribbon in the wind, so I add the other part of the ribbon.

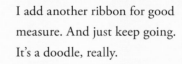

I add another ribbon for good measure. And just keep going. It's a doodle, really.

As I add more, I realize I need to see the ribbon, so I color that in with a Copic marker.

I keep creating little closed spaces that I can fill with color. I vary the size and shape of the images to add interest. The edges are painted black using a Marvy Fabric Marker.

Now it's time for coloring for professionals. Remember to hold your tongue just right and have fun. The colors will bleed, and you will probably put marker somewhere you wish you hadn't. Just keep going.

I add a little shading to the ribbon in a contrasting color using a fine-point Marvy Fabric Marker.

I add shading to the hearts using Gelato pigment sticks, tempera sticks, and STABILO Woody pencils with aloe.

It looks pretty chaotic to me at this point. I even contemplate giving up on it, but now I've named it and it's like a stray cat … once you name it, it's yours. I decide to delay my decision until it is completely colored in.

I'm glad I didn't give up. I am happy with it except for the dark blob near the upper right corner. That is a blob I cannot embrace. It really disrupts the unity of the piece. I'm going to try to rescue it using tempera sticks, Gelato pigment sticks, and a white uni-ball Signo pen. Nothing works. Maybe I just white the whole thing out and paint over it.

Yikes! That isn't going to work. It doesn't go with the rest of the piece. It stands out, and not in a good way. Sometimes this happens. You know what they say, "This happens." I think that's how it goes.

I can't live with this, so I do something radical. I decide to cut it out. I get out my Mistyfuse because it is almost unnoticeable on quilter's cotton. I apply a small piece of Mistyfuse that is slightly larger than the offending mess to the back of the piece. Then I use my tiny rotary cutter to surgically remove the offending part.

After I cut the piece out, I fuse a piece of white Kona cotton onto the back of the piece. It is the same fabric I used for the piece. I am careful to match the grain of the fabric as best I can. I use parchment paper under the piece so I don't fuse it to my drop cloth. I use parchment over the patch to protect my iron from any stray fusible.

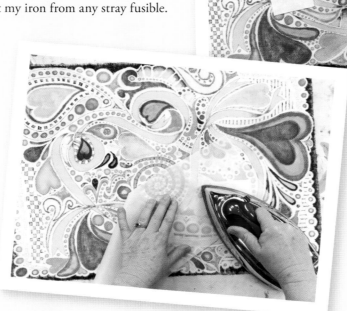

Good as new! Now I'm ready to add some checks with the black uni-ball Signo pen.

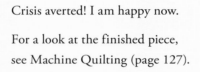

Crisis averted! I am happy now.

For a look at the finished piece, see Machine Quilting (page 127).

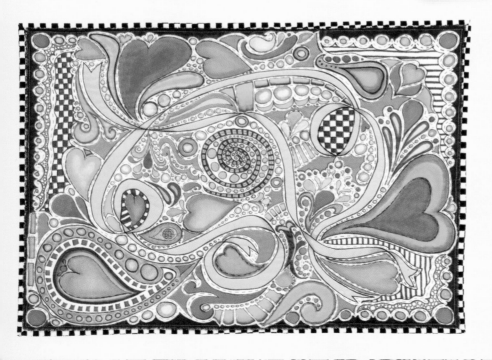

WYRD

Wyrd is painted with tempera crayons, Gelato pigment sticks, and STABILO Woody pencils. It is a good example of the allover-pattern composition map.

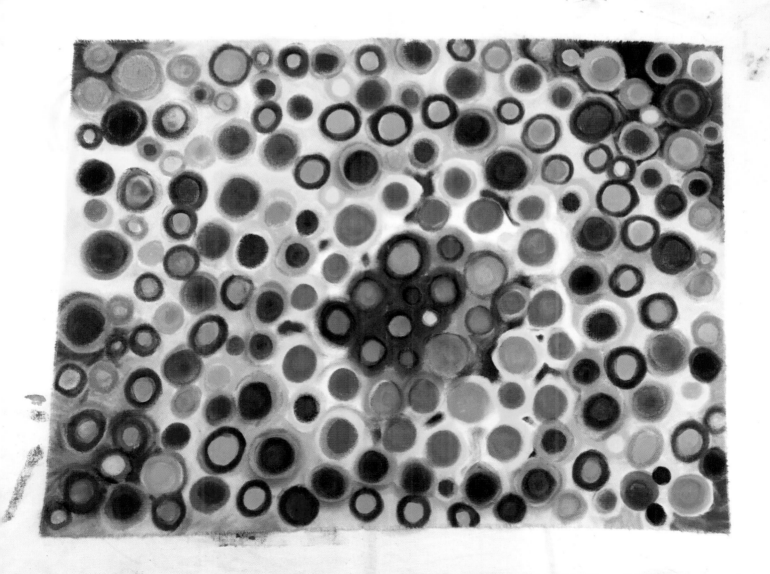

I start by drawing circles in the middle of the fabric using tempera sticks.

As I add circles, I think about color theory. Reds, oranges, and yellows (warm colors) abruptly change to cool colors. As I get the fabric filled, I go back in with a small stiff stencil brush and some aloe to blend a bit. I want the circles to look organic and have more than one color.

Yep, even this needs to be heat set.

I start adding Gelato pigment sticks to the piece, outlining the circles and filling in white space. Notice how I'm adding blue to the warm colors; this provides contrast. I go over some of the tempera circles to add more interest, and I blend it all with aloe and a stiff stencil brush.

I add some warm colors to the cool colors. This provides both unity and contrast.

For a look at the finished piece, see Gallery (page 134).

NOW WHAT?

A WORD ABOUT CREATIVITY

Often, it's necessary to take a break from a painting before deciding whether or not you're happy with it. Remember the old adage "you can't see the forest for the trees"? Art can be like that. Step back, give yourself some time, and revisit your newly finished painting. I must admit that I have cut up several paintings a bit prematurely. I am still happy with the squared painting, but looking back at photos of the whole paintings, sometimes I think the paintings are better than I thought at the time.

HOW TO KNOW YOU'RE FINISHED

Have a cup of tea, leave the room, and revisit your painting before you decide to cut it up. Trust your eye. I have a few little exercises that might help. Squint: That helps you see the whole composition without focusing on the parts. Use your phone and take a picture. Somehow that different perspective really helps. And finally, and this sounds weird, let the painting tell you if it's finished or not. I can't really describe it better than that. It will just somehow let you know if you take the time to stop and listen.

KEEP IT TOGETHER

Hole in the Wall

Some things to consider before you cut up your painting. First, no matter how great or how lacking, layering and stitching will add a lot to the painting. Layering provides structure, which traditional paintings have because they are generally on stretched canvas. Stitching adds texture.

It's hard to mimic how the
painting will look layered and
stitched. When trying to preview
the whole painting, I often lay
some thread across the top.
This doesn't really do the trick,
but it might give you an idea
if stitching will complete the
composition.

Another trick is to take a photo of
the painting, print it, and draw some
mock quilting on the paper. I use my
uni-ball Signo pens for this so I can
see them on the darker colors.

SQUARE IT OFF

Crown Jewels

Crown Jewels Squared

When the composition of the painting just isn't working, the rotary cutter or scissors swoop in to save the day. There really is something magical about cutting something up and putting it back together. I am always amazed at the mini masterpieces that emerge when I cut up a painting. I always find little compositional jewels that appear in an almost miraculous way.

A great way to decide if you want to cut up your painting is to use your printer, print a picture of your painting, and cut it up. I don't take time to be careful; I just dive in there with my (paper) scissors. I only need the idea to help me make a decision.

I didn't have to go far with *Europa and Her Sisters*. I have decided to keep the piece whole, layer it, and stitch it.

SLICE AND DICE

Here are a few tips if you decide to cut up your painting: It's a good idea to add fusible to the painting before you cut it up. Unless you plan on using a basting glue, it is very difficult to attach tiny little pieces of fusible to small squares of fabric. Please don't ask me how I know. Additionally, I like the stability the fusible gives the raw edges of the tiny little paintings. Sometimes I cut off the torn edge of the painting and sometimes I leave the fringe to add another element of variety to the squares.

This painting never made me happy. I decided I would cut it up early in the painting process, so I added lots of little extras to add interest to the squares.

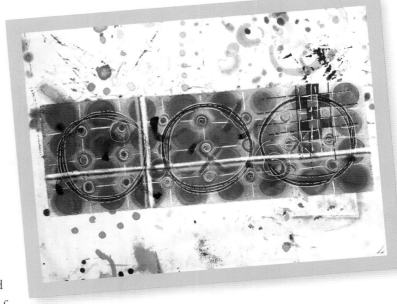

I like to use Lite Steam-A-Seam 2 (by The Warm Company), a double-stick light fusible that allows you to stick the squares down and move them before ironing them down permanently. It also allows the piece to be moved to the ironing surface without any squares jumping ship. Any fusible will work, but the double-stick properties of Lite Steam-A-Seam 2 make this fusible ideal for this process, as I can easily move the squares around multiple times until I am happy with the arrangement. I also really like the grid printed on the fusible backing. It makes deciding the square size and cutting easy.

Here's a secret: I don't worry too much about the squares being perfect. In fact, I like the results better with imperfect squares. If the painting is small, I use scissors to cut the squares. This ensures organic and imperfect squares. I think this makes the final product much more interesting.

If you use a fusible other than Lite Steam-A-Seam 2, remove the paper backing before cutting the squares. It can be tedious to remove the paper backing from all those little squares.

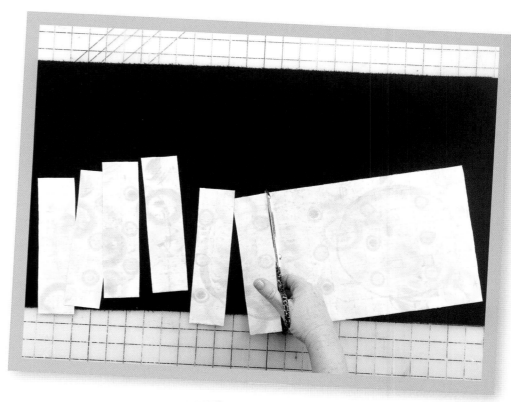

After cutting the squares, I mix them up a bit before I start placing them on the background.

In this example, I have used a piece of black quilting cotton. This is the fun part. I arrange and rearrange the squares until I am happy with the layout. This is where the double-stick fusible comes in handy.

In this case, I tear the fabric to size and place the squares. It took me a bit to decide exactly where on the black background I wanted the squares. I end up adjusting the size of the background a bit, and finally I'm happy and ready to use the iron to glue it down.

On *Kandinsky Kopied*, I decided to use black felt as the background for the squares. I buy the highest wool content I can find when I use this method. It is prettier than less expensive felt. I find it to be a bit more durable as well.

Kandinsky Kopied

TWEEDLE DO AND TWEEDLE DONE

A WORD ABOUT CREATIVITY

Finishing is not a strong suit for me. I have a hard time getting anything across the finish line. This is the point in the process that I fight the most resistance. All the fun is gone for me. So how do I do it? I tap into those six impossible things before breakfast. I remind myself that it's a gift to myself to finish. I am always so happy when I do. That said, I don't always finish right away. *Rabbit Moon* (page 142) has been in process for years! It is newly finished for this book.

Rabbit Moon Overview
Photo by Katie Fowler

MAKE THE PAINTING'S PRESENCE FELT

The fastest and easiest way to finish a painting is to baste it onto a piece of felt. I use felt with as much wool in it as I can get. It's worth the extra money because it is beautiful and much more durable—although these pieces will never be very durable.

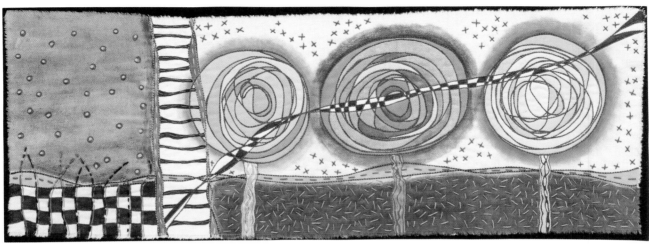

Orchard Ladder

I almost exclusively spray baste for this technique. I think spray baste is right up there with rotary cutters!

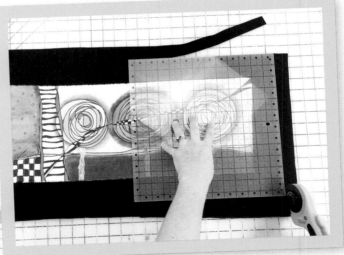

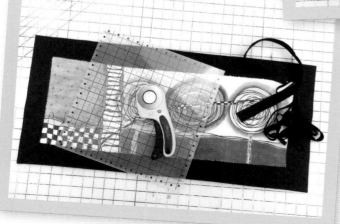

I find it's much easier to cut the felt *after* the painting is basted down. Then I don't have to try to center it. I find the straightest edge of the painting and square up the felt using that edge.

Now it's ready to stitch. I'll talk about that in Keep Calm and Stitch On (page 125).

WRAPPING IT UP

I learned this method of finishing a quilt from Susan Shie. I use it almost exclusively. I like it because it allows me to show the lovely raw edge of my torn fabric and requires very little precision. Very good for my style!

One of the best parts is choosing a background fabric. I have never started with a background fabric for a painting. It's always kind of a miracle how the right fabric just shows up. I found this fabric in my stash, and I love how the colors and pattern mimic the painting.

I determine how much of the backing fabric I want to show.

After spray basting the back side of the painting, I lay the painting faceup onto a piece of batting slightly larger than the painting. I use scissors to cut around the painting. You could use a rotary cutter and ruler if that makes you happier.

Next, I lay the painting and the batting on the wrong side of the backing fabric. The fabric should extend around the batting enough that it can be folded around the batting and tucked under the painting.

I tear the backing fabric to the appropriate size. Then I lift the spray-basted painting so I can tuck the backing fabric around the batting and under the painting and wrap the batting like a present. You can fold the fabric as a mitered corner or square to show the torn edge of the fabric.

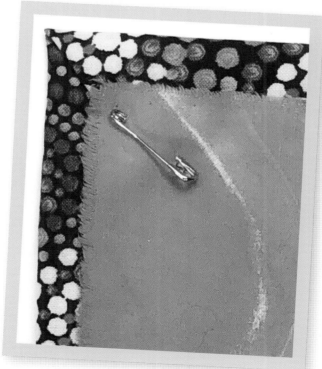

I usually miter the corners. Here, I've secured the fold with a basting pin.

Now I'm ready to stitch (see Keep Calm and Stitch On, page 125).

PILLOWCASE, QUILT, AND TOP-LIQUÉ

I use this method when I want a big variation in the amount of quilting in a piece. I want the background to have much more quilting than the cut-up painting. I learned this the hard way (like I learn most things) when I cut up a painting, put it on a whole piece of fabric, and quilted the border very heavily and the painting very lightly. That thing would never, ever lie flat.

This method serves two purposes: It allows the quilt to lie flat, and it provides an opportunity to make really beautiful fabric an important part of the piece. I have used traditional layering, quilting, and facing (bringing the binding entirely to the back of the quilt so it doesn't show). The advantage of this method is I can easily and neatly quilt off the edge.

I find that I get the same look if I pillowcase the quilt. It's faster and takes away a step I generally don't enjoy, hand stitching the binding. That's what I did on *Silicone Unction*.

I choose a background fabric and a backing fabric, both from my stash as well. It really is amazing and fun to find fabric that looks like it was made for your painting.

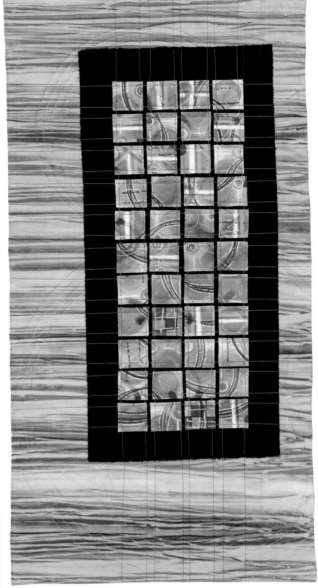

Silicone Unction

I lay the background and backing fabrics *right sides together* on top of the batting, which is slightly larger. I trim with my big square ruler right up to the fabric but leave extra fabric and batting at the opening. I throw a few pins in to keep the layers together.

I sew along the edge of the layers about ¼″ in all the way around, being sure to leave an opening where I left the extra batting and fabric. I make sure the opening is large enough to turn the layers right side out.

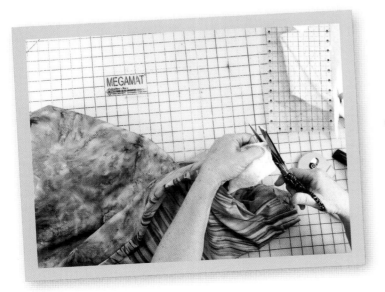

I trim the corners at a diagonal so they turn more cleanly.

I carefully turn the quilt right side out and flatten it, pressing if necessary and making sure all of the backing fabric is on the back. I love That Purple Thang (by Lynn Graves, Little Foot Ltd.) to carefully work the corners.

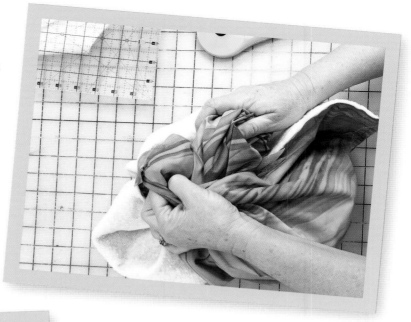

Once I am happy with the way the layers look, I fold back the extra fabric and trim *just the batting* to match the edge.

I carefully fold the fabric in on itself and sew it shut by machine. I continue to sew around the entire piece to help hold it in shape while I am quilting. This opening can also be stitched closed by hand if you don't want the stitching around the edges.

Now I'm ready to machine quilt the pillowcase sandwich. The edges are finished, so when I finish quilting and adding the painting, I'm all finished but for the sleeve.

KEEP CALM AND STITCH ON (OR QUILT AS DESIRED)

Disclaimer: I am not a quilting expert, and it's likely you know more about the right way to quilt than I do. The following is a brief demonstration of what I do.

Organic Hand Stitching

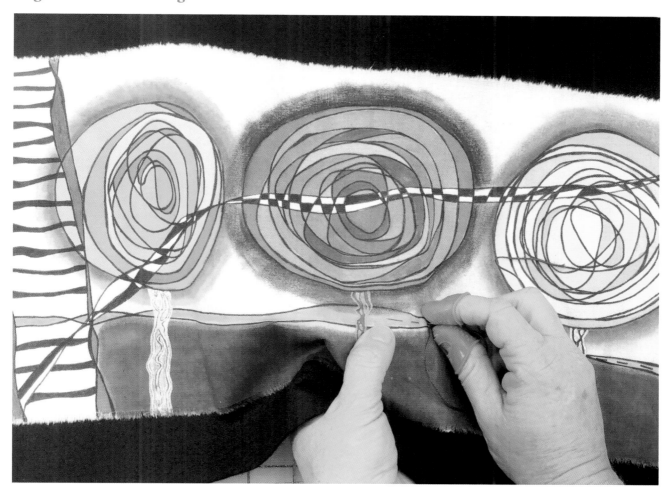

This piece was finished by basting it to felt and heavily hand stitching it with various sizes of perle cotton.

I hand stitch exclusively with perle cotton. I use a lot of WonderFil Eleganza, hand-dyed thread from Laura Wasilowski, Wildflowers thread (by The CARON Collection), Valdani, and anything else that catches my fancy. I have used thread from a number 12 (very thin) to a number 3 (fat and chunky).

The important thing to remember when quilting with heavy thread is to have the correct needle for the job. If the needle is to small for the thread, it will cause the thread to hang up on the layers and can cause the batting to beard, or poke through, the quilt top. Too large a needle will create a hole that may stay visible after the stitching is complete.

My rule of thumb is that if I can get the perle cotton through the eye of the needle fairly easily without it unwinding, then it's probably the right size. Experiment with different sizes and lengths of needles. You will soon find what is perfect for you. I like a longer needle so I can load it up with stitches.

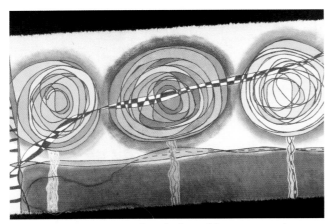

A big, chunky running stitch is the first of four go-to stitches.

Big, chunky French knots

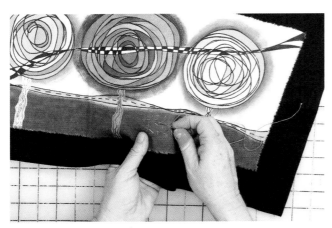

A big, chunky ricing stitch

Little X's

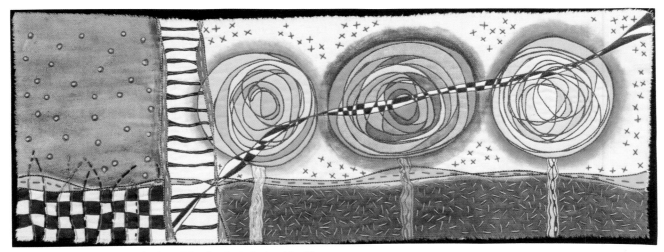

Remember: There are no rules here. The finished *Orchard Ladder*.

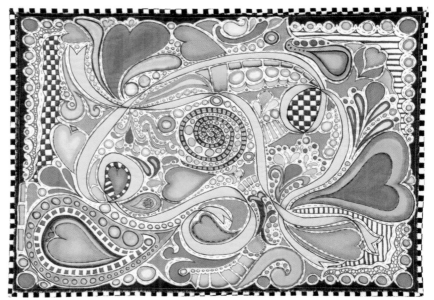

Machine Quilting

I like to mix up machine and hand stitching. I think it's unexpected and adds another element of interest to the piece.

Mad Hatter's Love Letter

Europa and Her Sisters

I have done both free-motion quilting and walking-foot quilting. There are a lot of books and experts who can teach this better than I can.

Here are a few examples of how I have combined machine and hand stitching.

Self-Portrait Copenhagen

Drouk Love

Whichever method you choose to finish your piece, enjoy it. Accept it as your own unique piece of art, and let go of the critical voice if you have one.

Idunn's Orchard

OH NO! I STILL DON'T LIKE IT!

A WORD ABOUT CREATIVITY

An art professor once told me that what we create isn't precious. I'm not sure I totally agree with that. I don't really like to sell my pieces; I like to keep them. I like to keep them because I can always remake something with them. They are like my stash. I've been told that means I'm not a real artist. Seriously? How many rules do I have to follow to be a real artist? Actually, none. There are no rules. I create to express myself because I love to create and because it makes me feel whole. I don't care if I'm really an artist or not. So, in one way, my quilts aren't precious because I like to cut them up. On the other hand, I really like to look at them, touch them, and remember where I was in life when I made them.

CUT IT UP!

It's layered and it's quilted, and you still don't love it. That's okay! This is a zero-stress book. Cut it up! Once you put it back together, you'll like it. The great thing about this as a last (or intentional) resort is that all that quilting goes back together in a mishmash way and looks really great.

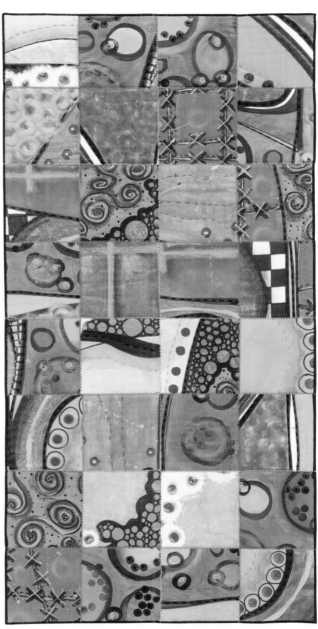

Rebel

Bird's Eye View
Photo by Katie Fowler

Here are the steps to take to make what I call a "humpty-dumpty quilt."

1. Lay your finished quilt on your cutting table.

2. Decide how big you want the squares to be.

3. Walk away if you're not sure.

4. Take a deep breath.

5. Cut.

The pieces are a bit fragile at this point, so handle them with gentle hands.

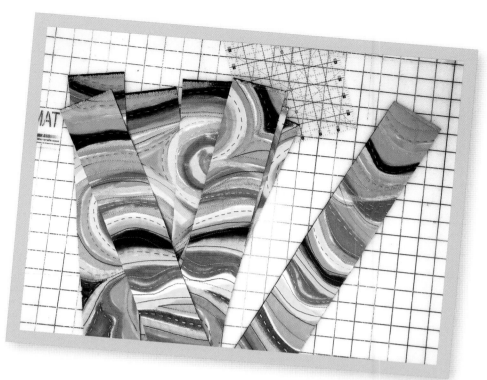

PUT YOUR QUILT TOGETHER AGAIN

It won't take "all the king's horses and all the king's men" to put your quilt together again. Play with the little mini masterpieces you have created. Arrange them so you are happy. The other option is to appliqué them to a background like I have done here.

Sew them together using a zigzag stitch or a decorative stitch of your choice. Butt the edges together and stitch.

Remember that we are not seeking perfection. This may not be perfect. Light can shine through some of my humpty-dumpty quilts. The bigger ones are harder to get lined up exactly right than the smaller ones. I'm probably never going to win any traditional quilting awards, and that's okay with me. I just want to have fun and be happy with the final project.

THE DREAMER RETURNS

Alice's Adventures in Wonderland ends with Alice awakening from her fantastical dreams. Then Alice's older sister falls asleep and begins to dream about the characters from Alice's adventure. This is how Alice's sister wakes up:

> Lastly, she pictured to herself how this same little sister of hers would, in the after-time, be herself a grown woman; and how she would keep, through all her riper years, the simple and loving heart of her child-hood: and how she would gather about her other little children, and make their eyes bright and eager with many a strange tale, perhaps even with the dream of Wonderland long ago: and how she would feel with all their simple sorrows, and find a pleasure in all their simple joys, remembering her own child-life, and the happy summer days.

The magic found in the creative process isn't found in the reality of a thing. This magic is found in the imagination. The infinite possibility of imagination is the true gift of being creative. If we are human, we are creative. Read again what Alice's sister says: Alice would "be herself a grown woman; and how she would keep, through all her riper years, the simple and loving heart of her child-hood." It is the infinite possibility that draws me to my studio again and again. I am where I belong when my imagination prompts my every move. I feel energized, worthy, and whole in that space.

Zen Bunny

It is this surrender to childlike wonder that fuels my creativity. Everything is possible in that place where I lose track of time and space. When I am stuck and not finding my creative groove, I try to remember my "childlife," wandering through the field near our house and finding odd bits and pieces. Imagining what they might become. I remember the sheer delight of opening a brand-new box of 64 crayons. The wonder I felt when that first piece of copper enamel came out of the oven in art class. The love affair with art and rock and roll that began in eighth grade art class when Mrs. Shoe allowed us to listen to records.

Please Turn It Down!

Today, it's all about surrender. Letting go of my expectations, my perfectionism, and my fears. Learning and using tools to get past resistance and procrastination. Using my inner strength to battle self-doubt, negativity, and creative chaos.

I hope you will have the courage to follow that white rabbit and go down the rabbit hole. Find the place that is your Wonderland. Surrender yourself to the experience of possibilities, for that is where the magic can be found.

The Fool

GALLERY

Digression, 23″ × 33″, wholecloth painting squared

Mad Hatter's Convergence, 22½″ × 22½″, computer-generated, hand-painted mandala cut up
and put back together using Ricky Tims' Convergence technique

Tresillo, 29″ × 29″, hand-drawn and colored mandala

Morocco, 25″ × 25″, hand-drawn and colored mandala.

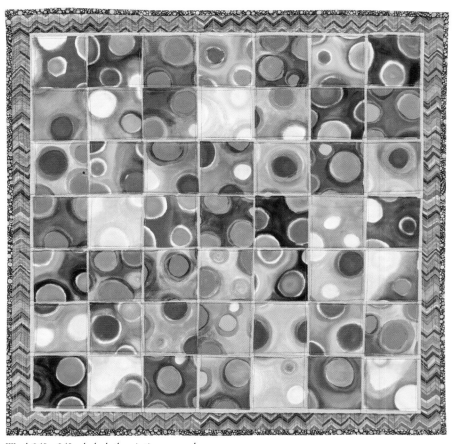

Wyrd, 24″ × 24″, wholecloth painting squared

Self-Portrait Florence, 38″ × 28″, wholecloth painting

Self-Portrait Rome, 38″ × 25″, wholecloth painting

Interval Unhinged, 16″ × 16″, wholecloth painting

Evora, 26″ × 26″, wholecloth painting

Ruby Diadem, 11″ × 21″, wholecloth painting squared

Tiny Garden, 12″ × 14½″, wholecloth painting squared

Checkmate; 30″ × 30″; hand-colored, original computer-generated mandalas; machine appliqué

Syncretism, 16″ × 42″, wholecloth painting squared

Square Pegs, 45″ × 45″, wholecloth painting

Rabbit Moon, 45″ × 45″, wholecloth painting

ABOUT THE AUTHOR

Katie Fowler lives in the foothills of Colorado with her husband, Bill. She began quilting in 1997 when her kids were little. Katie discovered art quilting early on in her quilting career when she realized she couldn't follow directions. She has been a maker her whole life and a teacher her whole adult life. She has a hard time focusing on just one type of making, but mark-making on fabric has truly become a passion. Katie's intention is to find that happy place in her studio when time loses all meaning. She hopes this book helps you find that, too.

Katie loves all things color and creativity. She is fascinated by color theory and helps people to understand it is a tool, not a rule. She is a certified Kaizen-Muse Creativity Coach and uses her experience to help others find their creative bliss. It is important to her that people enjoy what they are doing. Katie likes to give people permission to play and help them find their unique childlike creative play. Having wrestled with the creative process most of her life, she knows the ups and downs very well. It's not about "coloring outside the lines;" it's about finding what you love. Coloring inside the lines is okay if that's what you love, and so is coloring outside the lines—or even a little bit of both. Katie wants you to do what makes you happy.

Photo by Katie Fowler

Visit Katie online and follow on social media!

Website: katiefowler.net

Facebook: /createcurious

Pinterest: /ktfowlerquilts

Instagram: @katiefowlerwonderland

Also by Katie Fowler: